Creative Media Resources
P.O. Box   1665
Sandpoint, ID 83864
1-800-858-9388

CONNECTING

With The

POWER OF GOD

S0-DQW-249

CONNECTING

With the

POWER OF GOD

Hilmar Von Campe

Dandridge Hall Press, Inc.
P.O. Box 31655
Lafayette, La 70593

ISBN 1-888627-01-8

ORIGINAL COVER ART BY: GINNY PARKER

CONTENTS

ACKNOWLEDGMENTS

I owe a great debt of gratitude to my wife Dina, whose enduring faith and support were crucial for my being able to be true to my calling and to write this book. I am very grateful also to my sister Sibylle and my brother-in-law Hans Heidrich whose help and active engagement played a decisive part in making this book possible. I also wish to thank Dr. Craig W. Nickisch, who was kind enough to read the draft manuscript, and whose many helpful suggestions, both in language and content, have contributed immeasurably to the volume. Any errors or omissions, of course, are my own.

I owe special acknowledgment to the late Dr. Frank N.D. Buchman, founder of Moral Rearmament, whose life, thinking and vision for a world under God influenced greatly my own thinking and outlook on the world which is reflected in this book. I am also endebted to the late British journalist, author and statesman Peter Howard who liberated me and my mother from our hatred of the British and taught me that any hatred is not only wrong and self-destructive but dumb. He showed me how to replace it with compassion, love and fight for what is right. Finally, this book would not have been possible without Artur Richter who started me out into a new life of obedience to my creator.

THE PROPHESY OF ST. NILUS
5th Century Hermit

Nilus, an early Christian monk who died about 430 A.D., was abbot of a monastery in Ankara (now Turkey), who later became a hermit in the Sinai. He was highly regarded as an advisor and maintained an active correspondence.

"After the year 1900, toward the middle of the 20th century, people will become unrecognizible. When the time for the Advent of the Antichrist approaches, people's minds will grow cloudy from carnal passions, and dishonor and lawlessness will grow stronger. Then the world will become unrecognizible. People's appearances will change, and it will be impossible to distinguish men from women due to their shamelessness in dress and style of hair. These people will be cruel and will be like wild animals because of the temptations of the Antichrist. There will be no respect for parents and elders, love will disappear, and Christian pastors, bishops and priests will become vain men, failing completely to distinguish the right hand way from the left. At that time the morals and traditions of Christians and of the Church will change. People will abandon modesty, and dissipation will reign. Falsehood and greed will attain great proportions, and woe to those who pile up treasures. Lust, adultery, homosexuality, secret deeds and murder will rule society.

At that future time, due to the power of such great crimes and licentiousness, people will be deprived of the grace of the Holy Spirit, which they received in Holy Baptism and equally of remorse.

The churches of God will be deprived of God-fearing pious pastors, and woe to the Christians remaining in the world at that time; they will completely lose their faith because they will lack the opportunity of seeing the light of knowledge from anyone at all. Then they will separate themselves out of the world in holy refuges in search of lightening their spiritual sufferings, but everywhere they will meet obstacles and constraints. And all of this will result from the fact that the Antichrist wants to be Lord over everything and become the ruler of the whole universe, and he will produce miracles and fantastic signs. He will also give depraved wisdom to an unhappy man so that he will discover a way by which one man can carry on a conversation with another from the end of the earth to the other. At that time men will also fly through the air like birds and descend to the bottom of the sea like fish. And when they have achieved all this, these unhappy people will spend their lives in comfort without knowing, pour souls, that it is the deceit of the Antichrist. And the impious one, He will so infuse science with vanity that it will go off the right path and lead people to lose faith in the existence of God in three hypostases.

The All Good God will see the downfall of the human race and will shorten the days for the sake of those few who will be saved, because the enemy wants to lead even the chosen into temptation, if that is possible... the sword of chastisement will suddenly appear and kill the perverter and his servants."

FOREWORD

As a prologue to this volume, I suggest the reader consider these quotes from great thinkers of the past:

"We have staked the whole future of American civilization, not upon the power of government, far from it. We have staked the future of all our political institutions upon the capacity of mankind for self-government; upon the capacity of each and all of us to govern ourselves, to sustain ourselves according to the Ten Commandments of God."

> *- James Madison*
> *(Christian Crusade Newspaper, October, 1995)*

"The longer I live, the more convincing proofs I see that God governs in the affairs of men. (Without God's) concurring aid we shall succeed in this political building no better than the builders of Babel."

> *- Benjamin Franklin*
> *(Constitutional Convention in Philadelphia, 28 June 1787)*

"Almighty God, we make our earnest prayer that Thou wilt keep the United States in Thy holy protection, ... that Thou wilt most graciously be pleased to dispose us all to do justice, to love mercy, and to demean ourselves with that charity, humility, and pacific temper of mind which were the characteristics of the Divine Author of our blessed religion, and without an humble imitation of whose example in these things, we can never hope to be a happy nation. Grant our supplication, we beseech Thee, through Jesus Christ our Lord. Amen."

- George Washington
(Prayer for The Nation, Newburg, 8 June 1783)

"I have sworn upon the altar of God eternal hostility against every form of tyranny over the mind of man."

- Thomas Jefferson
(In a letter to Benjamin Rush, 23 September 1800)

"It is Religion and Morality alone which can establish the principles upon which freedom can securely stand. A patriot must be a religious man."

- John Adams
(*The Naked Public Square,* Richard John Newhaus)

"The highest glory of the American Revolution was this, to be connected in one indissoluble bond the principles of civil government with the principles of Christianity".

-John Quincy Adams
"The Flight from America's Foundations: A Panoramic Perspective on American Law" (Restoring the Constitution, Virginia Armstrong)

"We have been the recipients of the choicest bounties of Heaven; we have grown in numbers, wealth, and power as no other nation has ever grown. But we have forgotten God. We have forgotten the gracious hand which preserved us in peace and multiplied and enriched and strengthened us, and we have vainly imagined, in the deceitfulness of our hearts, that all these blessings were produced by some superior wisdom and virtue of our own. Intoxicated with unbroken success, we have become so self-sufficient to feel the necessity of redeeming and preserving grace, too proud to pray to the God that made us.

It behoves us, then, to humble ourselves before the offended

Power, to confess our national sins, and to pray for clemency and forgiveness... All this being done in sincerity and truth, let us then rest humble in the hope authorized by the divine teachings that the united cry of the nation will be heard on high and answered with blessings no less than the pardon of our national sins and the restoration of our now divided and suffering country to its former happy condition of unity and peace.

In witness whereof I have hereunto set my hand and caused the seal of the United States to be affixed."

- Abraham Lincoln
(The city of Washington, 30 March, 1863)

"We believe that the ultimate purpose in living is to know and glorify God and to attain eternal life through Jesus Christ our Lord, beginning within our own families and then reaching out to a suffering humanity that does not know of His love and sacrifice.

We believe that human life is of inestimable worth and significance in all its dimensions, including the aged, the widowed, the mentally handicapped, the unattractive, the physically challenged, and every other condition in which humanness is expressed from conception to the grave."

- James Dobson
(Focus on the Family, Statement of Policy)

The following is a letter published by the author in several U.S. newspapers at the occasion of the 50 years celebration of the end of World War II and the liberation of the surviving inmates of Nazi concentration camps.

"The atrocity and inhumanity of the Holocaust was the extreme consequence of the arrogance of man, of human beings, who set themselves up above all others, despising the value of human life. The then executive director of the Holocaust Memorial Council in Washington, Rabbi Dr. David Weinstein, received me twice and I apologized to him for the suffering Germany had inflicted on the Jewish people. I told Rabbi Weinstein that the crimes of the Nazis were only possible because of the moral cowardice of so many of us non-Nazis. We Christians, the so-called good people, had a relative morality and only small personal goals.

The opportunists outnumbered by far the men of the resistance who paid with their lives for opposing Hitler and his gang. Remembering the Holocaust the focus should be on the bystanders and the appeasers of evil who were silent when faced at the beginning of the process with discrimination and injustice commited against others. It was not God who let the Holocaust happen. It was us who rejected His Commandments.

My father died in a Soviet concentration camp no less inhuman than the Nazi camps. I have forgiven the Poles and the Russians as I need forgiveness myself. If the suffering of millions of people is to have any meaning, it can only be the lesson that out of guilt and suffering, a spirit of forgiveness, reconciliation, and common destiny can arise, leading in turn to the birth of a new human society where humanity obeys the laws of its Creator. Before the Holocaust was the evil spirit of hatred, class- and race-war, abuse of power, and despising of human life. My restitution for the atrocities commited by a German government in the name of Germany is the commitment of my life to fight this spirit of evil in whatever form it appears in whatever part of the world so that the truth of God can be established who commands us to love our neighbors as ourselves."

When we remember the nightmares of those years with their repercussions throughout the whole world, proclaiming that we will never let it happen again, why then is it that the American and European governments, media and people are silent with regard to the Tibetan Holocaust? Communist China, a member of the Security Council of the United Nations, has been brutally and systematically attempting to eliminate a whole people and a whole culture, murdering so far 1.3 million people, which represents a third of the population.

"I know what you have done, and that you are neither cold nor hot. I could wish that you were either cold or hot. But since you are lukewarm and neither cold nor hot, I intend to spit you out of my mouth."

Revelations 3:15

CHAPTER 1

PREPARING THE ARGUMENT

Theologians and philosophers such as Aristotle, St. Thomas of Aquinas, Descartes, Kant, Kierkegaard, Nietzsche, Sartre, Tillich and countless others have disputed among themselves for centuries, filled thousands of pages, one explanation is more complicated than the other, on how to prove or disprove the existence of God. I believe that their approaches lack some basic ingredients. It may be compared to philosophizing today about whether or not electricity exists. You switch on your lamp, and once connected with the current it shines. Therewith you have demonstrated the existence of electricity and everybody can see it. You cannot see the electricity, of course, but you can see the light of the lamp. That is the proof. Of course nowadays everybody has a theoretical knowledge about electricity before switching on the light. The same is true for God. In America 96 percent of the people say that they believe in God. On the following pages therefore I shall prove the existence of God in the same way. Metaphorically speaking, consider yourself to be the lamp and God to be electricity. The lamp does nothing—it simply shines. Similarly, in the case of God and you, this shining is not a question of doing or having the right arguments but of being.

Many of us confuse our intellectual knowledge about God and of religious doctrines with faith. In the case of philosophers and theologians that leads to extreme complications and intellectual contortions, which make life difficult, especially for students. My daughter Sabrina took a correspondence course named "Philosophy and Theology" from the University of Colorado at Boulder. The author of the course, who holds philosophical and theological academic degrees, differentiates between revealed and philosophical theology. I went with my daughter through every page of that course and at the end we asked ourselves, "so what?" It would be much simpler to just study the Bible and relate the truth found there, not just in terms of one's own existence, but to society and foreign policy, for that matter. So I sought to clarify what remained unresolved in that philosophy and theology course.

I am neither philosopher nor theologian, but neither were the first Christians, including the Apostles, yet their beliefs obviously had priority over their job security, otherwise why would they be so foolish as to let themselves be thrown to the lions?

Some years ago I asked a professor of theology, an expert in Christian sociology, where precisely in the Bible I could find what Jesus had said about loving God with all your heart and all your strength and all your soul. He said, "How would I know? You must ask your parish priest." So much for theologians.

Theology concerns the knowledge of God and philosophy tries rationally to explain the reality of the world and the reason for the existence of man. But most of the theologians and philosophers are like teachers who eloquently explain the composition of H_2O but don't know the taste of water nor have they ever been in a swimming pool. I would add a third concept: experimental theology. You don't need to go to a university to learn about it either. The master's degree will be the knowledge of God as he will reveal himself to you and explain your reason for existence as you advance through life, obedient to his commandments. This road which I shall explain in the course of this essay naturally is also open for theologians and philosophers, even for politicians. And I hope that, from their present vantage point, St. Thomas and St. Augustin will not raise their eyebrows at my systematics.

There is an assault on Christian values in America. Values are being ridiculed especially in the media and in Hollywood films. In a Bible class in Colorado Springs, which I attend when I am in the city, some people talk about the persecution which Christians suffer from politicians, schools and courts. All of this is certainly a reality and reminds me very much of Nazi-Germany which I experienced as a boy. The Republican landslide in the elections of the 8th of November 1994 was of course to a large extent the consequence of Christian voters being fed up with a leadership which fosters immorality, tries to eliminate God's relevance in society and push Him into a private religious corner.

But what was it in the first place which led to a situation in the freest country on earth, founded by Christians, in which Christians consider themselves to be persecuted? Where they seem to be completely irrelevant in determining the rules for social behavior in their own country while their government is busy lecturing other countries on social behavior and trying to force, in many cases, its own non-Christian views upon them, either directly or via the United Nations. Therefore in the course of this essay I shall deal with the root cause of this development which I might call "the American religious flu." "When the Gentiles, who have no knowledge of the Law, act in accordance with it by the light of nature, they show that they have a law in themselves, for they demonstrate the effect of a law operating in their own hearts. Their own consciences endorse the existence of such a law, for there is something which condemns or commends their actions,"[1] wrote St. Paul in the second chapter of his letter to the Romans. The German philosopher Immanuel Kant developed what is called the "Moral Argument," with which he wanted to prove rationally the existence of God. The essence of this argument is that each person has an objective moral law within himself, which is independent of his own opinions or inclinations. The origin of this moral law and the source of the moral consciousness must be God, "the supreme being", argues Kant, who though, since he was a philosopher, failed like most of his colleagues to make it practical. Rene Descartes, a 17th century French philosopher, deducted from his knowledge, about his own lack of moral perfection, that there must be an infinite perfection as a yardstick for his imperfections, a "most perfect being," somebody who is without any fault—God. Centuries before them St. Thomas Aquinas had pointed out, in the fourth of his famous five ways to prove the existence of God, that since human morality as practiced in this world is relative (more or less good, more or less true, more or less noble, etc.) there had to be an absolute being by which the relativity can be measured. The absolute must be God, he stated.

Let's look at the issue from the other side. Theologians and philosophers like Bultmann, Heidegger, Nietzsche, Satre, Camus and those of the "death of God theology" deny the existence and reality of God. Asked whether he believes in the resurrection of Jesus Christ, Bultmann replied, "I am a theologian, not an archeologist."[2] Satre's philosophical point of departure is that there is no God and therefore no ultimate frame of reference, no absolute and eternal truth. The world to him is meaningless and absurd. "The dignity and meaning of man lie in his unyielding resolve against the absurd," adds Camus as his contribution to the understanding of life.[3] The point, though, which becomes apparent in the argumentation of these nihilists is the close connection between the rejection of God and the simultaneous rejection of absolute morality—Christian morality. They are miserable and see neither hope nor meaning in life because of their personal immorality which of course is reflected in their philosophies. In other words "morality first, philosophy second." Not intellect, not intelligence but morality determines the thinking of a person.

That is why we have to view the morality of people in government, especially when they come up with bombastic and expensive schemes. This point was made clear by Aldous Huxley, a contemporary British author, who started out like Satre but changed later on in his life becoming honest about what made him tick. "I had motives for not wanting the world to have a meaning, consequently assumed that it had none, and was able without any difficulty to find satisfying reasons for this assumption... For myself, as no doubt for most of my contemporaries, the philosophy of meaninglessness was essentially an instrument of liberation. The liberation we desired was simultaneously liberation from a certain political and economic system and liberation from a certain system of morality. We objected to the morality because it interfered with our sexual freedom." This means that very often, perhaps even in the majority of cases, intellectual argumentation is nothing but shadowboxing, because the reasons given are intellectual smoke screens which hide real intentions. The underlying moral reality must be addressed. In the case of people who call themselves social progressives, it normally can be summarized as: free sex and other people's property.

In the moral field there are both absolute and relative standards. Absolute moral standards can only be derived from absolute truth and only God is absolute truth. Since God created all people (and not only Christians!) It can safely be assumed that he set the same moral laws for all of them. Could it be that he also has a purpose for the world he created, a kind of master plan? In the same way as an architect who builds a house, could it be that the realization of this purpose, this master plan, depends on you and me, on all men and women, obeying the moral imperatives within ourselves? Looking at the world of today one can only conclude that it must be our leaders disobedience to the truth inside that led to and produced the dangerous mess we are in and which, I am convinced, is contrary to what God wants for us. Instead of divisive arguing about doctrines (as we see among Christians and especially among theologians today) and trying to convert each other to "my true beliefs," it would be much more sensible to work together for the implementation of God's moral laws, which most world religions have in common, independent of whether one recognizes God as Creator or not.

God is a moral force and His revelations are commands of moral nature and not descriptions of heaven or of how to realize one's self. There is no way to find God outside His absolute morality. Newt Gingrich is right when he said at the occasion of his installation as Speaker of the House on 4 January 1995 that America is facing a moral crisis which has to be dealt with as such. Why then is it that you hear so little about it from the pulpits across the country? Are Christian leaders out of step with reality? Finally, does the command, "Thou shall love thy neighbor as thyself" apply to individuals only or also to governments which represent those individuals, and in the case we discuss here, does it apply to the American government? If the law of God is in the best interest of the people (i.e. of each individual) that seems to ask the question: what then is the definition of "national interest" which a government is obliged to pursue?

CHAPTER 2

BLAMING GOD

"You cannot eliminate the problem of earthquakes, floods, etc. by making a distinction between bad and evil and refusing to allow the expression natural evil. That is just a verbal quibble: the fact remains that earthquakes and floods do great harm to innocent victims and that God, being omnipotent, should be able to prevent them if he wanted to (and should want to, since he is good)," according to the liberal professor of Sabrina's correspondence course from the University of Colorado. She gave Sabrina a lower grade than usual for she had stated in her essay that the distinction of "Natural Evil" as a form of evil beside "Personal Evil" logically leads to the conclusion that God is to blame for evil, exempting therewith man from the consequences of his sins. She also took exception to the concept put forth by the author of the course, that the antithesis of evil is good. It should be godly, she stated (or righteous, I might add). Bad and evil are not the same, evil comes from within every human being, she said, "an act of the free will, a rebellion against God," as St. Augustine explained. It is interesting to note in this context that even "natural" disasters can turn out to be man made. At the beginning of 1995 hundreds of thousands of people in Europe were threatened by flooding, as rains caused the Rhine river to flood vast areas of Germany and Holland. It was then argued by scientists that human modifications to the bed of the river over many decades (to make it easier to navigate) gave the water a destructive force which it otherwise would not have had.

The Boulder professor, though, did not agree with my daughter's argument. It would have been all right, I suppose, to include Christian views in the argument as the author of the course did, as long as one did not insist on them, and on the other side gave an equal weight to the wishy-washy reasoning of most of these mediocre philosophers like David Hume and Jean Paul Sartre, to name only a few of the legion.

But if you do that you have already left the Christian moral ground and have moved into an area where all things are equal. And that is precisely what is being taught at many universities. There is nothing wrong in discussing the views of those philosophical and theological celebrities as long as you are firmly rooted in your Christian soil of absolute morality and know that the thinking of a person and his world view are determined by his morality. Since Christian values have been eroded in the last decades, there are not many students who will stand their ground, and parents have to be cautious as to which university and to what classes they send their children (and their *money*).

Once you accept the underlying principle that all things are equal you are on the easy road to moral compromise and immorality. Take the case of David Bonior, the minority whip in the House of Representatives, who started out as pro-life, then stated that he personally is pro-life but politically he would go with the pro-choice orientation of the Democratic Party. That of course was more convenient for his career. He ended up voting seventy-one percent for the abortion agenda, which means protecting and making murder legal. Bonior tried to convince his colleagues to do the same. Still he considers himself to be a Christian like so many other confused Americans. It is "either-or," you can't be for murder and for Jesus at the same time. Think about it for a moment. If you have people leading any country who call murder a choice, in what direction are they leading their country? Would it be the same direction Germany went under Hitler?

My daughter and of course all other students are subjected to a world of "equality." Teachers take on the appearance of being objective scholars, but in reality they are not. A great many are no different from the liars in the mainstream media, who disguise themselves as objective journalists, but push their own liberal views disguised as news or reports. The same happens with universities and if you stand firm, as Sabrina did because she received her parent's education, you run the risk of receiving lower grades. Liberals do not hesitate to pressure the students to give ground for the sake of better grades, which in turn affect their overall academic standing with the consequent qualifications for scholarships or not, student aid, and all the rest of it.

What started out in this chapter as a matter of different philosophical views turns out to reach into the very existence of our family. For Sabrina, who has a high grade point average, standing by her belief puts her in danger. The consequence could be lowering her academic standing, which she understandably wants to avoid. For me encouraging her to do so and helping her with her argumentation means that I might have to pay more for her education. This does not make me very enthusiastic considering the financial difficulties any family faces while children are in college.

Let me then pose the following question: if Sabrina would have aimed at higher grades by trying to please her teacher, who would be responsible for her abandoning her own beliefs? Sabrina? Or, the pressure of the environment represented by the teaching establishment? Would it be correct to blame God for allowing such a situation to exist since he is omnipotent? In any case, my daughter stuck to her guns and her teacher was a much better person than I had thought at the beginning. Sabrina received a reasonably objective grade from the professor.

Nobody can choose the environment he is born into. You can neither choose your parents nor your name. Some are born into a wealthy western family, others into an Indian slum. One is white, the other black, the next yellow; one is born from a Christian, the next from Islamic parents, while the parents of a third child may be atheists or God-haters. One child grows up on a peaceful Pacific island while the other endures bombing raids in the middle of war and destruction. One child is born outside marriage and never sees her father while another one is brought up by loving and united parents and a third one grows up in a family where parents fight all the time, beat the child frequently and do not give it much attention. Is God unjust? Has the government to correct this injustice? For instance, does the government take money from the wealthy western father to give it to the slum dweller so that everybody has an equal income?

Without any doubt the environment which nobody can influence at the beginning of his life has a decisive impact on the character and concepts of every human being. Obviously the conditions for the take-off to life are so unequal, if not unjust, that it is impossible to compensate the less-favored here on earth in such a way that equality is achieved and one's sense of justice is satisfied.

When I was 10 years old I was ordered into the Hitler Youth, according to German law at that time, and exposed to organized state corruption. Others, because of another law, had to be members of the Red Pioneers and exposed to a similar state corruption. The lucky ones could choose to become members of the Boy or Girl Scouts, but a growing number of them at the same time were being offered condoms and related education in their schools and exposed to yet another form of state corruption. Is the last mentioned corruption perhaps not quite as bad as the previous two? Are those of us who were born into a Christian environment the righteous ones? Are we better and closer to God than the others? Can we just enjoy our status, try to be good and be the saved since we know about Jesus Christ while the poor pagans, like for instance the Hindus, are walking on the path to hell? A child grows up in a given environment and eventually becomes conscious of social and state structures. These were established by other people and are represented by officials who try to enforce them. Normally reasons are offered for the justification of those rules, which are always supposed to be of benefit to people. I don't know of any laws and regulations which state that they are mainly for the benefit of those who made them! But since a great many of them certainly are, the question of hypocrisy arises, and with it the question of how to deal with it. Normally disobedience to laws is punished. In some nations you are told what to think, what is politically correct, and if you dare to utter different views you can lose your life or in milder cases your career. What then is the fundamental difference between a democratic and a totalitarian society? It is the margin, not the essence of freedom.

In face of all these outside influences on his life the challenge for the individual is how to cope with it. Has he to accept what is imposed upon him or has he to oppose it? Can, or must, he influence the environment? Wouldn't it be the wisest to arrange oneself with the powers that be in order to avoid trouble and pursue unmolested one's personal aims? Does one not have the right to expect those powers to solve one's problems of existence, or to guarantee for instance a minimum of security? Is man, upon reaching the age of an adult, a product of society and of the environment he could not influence? Are his actions mere consequences of it, and is he therefore not responsible (or perhaps only partly responsible) for what he does? If my parents beat me regularly is it justifiable if I kill them, or take it out on somebody else, or do I still have to love them as God commands? Has man the power to break the stranglehold of a given environment and can he even change it?

The scale of possible behaviors towards power in all its forms within society lies between two poles of philosophy. One was packaged into a set of social and economic doctrines by Karl Marx, which then was called *Marxism*. The other was taught by Jesus. When I say this I am not upgrading Marx to the level of Jesus, or comparing them as equals. Because Marx has reached such prominence, his doctrines only serve as a good example for a philosophy presented in many disguises. This philosophy denies individual responsibility and blames others for what is wrong. It uses and magnifies that wrong to cover up one's own immorality. The essence of all of Marx' theories is this thesis that society and unjust structures are controlled by the rich. That means that others are responsible for the dissatisfying state of affairs in the world. Socialist thinking exploits the human tendency to feel like a victim of someone or something, to whitewash and justify ones own behavior and blame others for ones own faulty or doubtful actions. Equipped with Marxist philosophy, one can indignantly crusade against the evil of others without contributing a thing towards finding a solution. Those who shift the blame to others as the basis of their philosophy, as a rule, reject God. How do they reject God? Not necessarily by denying him intellectually, or by words, but always by liberating themselves from the demands of absolute morality.

You recognize the godless by what they do, and not necessarily by what they say. It is a strange fact in human nature that the feeling of being wronged, the overture to hatred, gives a person the satisfying sense of being right and a cause to live by. If you start to attack those who gave you these feelings, you find that there is no person and no nation which has not been wronged by somebody else—some nations all the time. In the world of today there is a growing generation of hatred. And to the same degree that moral restraints disappear, the capacity to deal with resentment and hatred disappears too. While politicians refuse to address the issue, the danger of destruction rises. The riots in Los Angeles and the bomb in Oklahoma reflect that growing trend.

Jesus on the other hand teaches that each human being is not only responsible for himself or herself and for the consequences of their own action, but also for their fellow human beings. Compliance with God's commandments which Jesus expects from everybody, not just from Christians, are not meant to result in the perfection of those who take them seriously in order to get to heaven, as many members of religious denominations wrongly believe. God's commandments are aimed at the satisfaction of the vital needs of others. That is why the commandments, to love God with all your heart and then to love your neighbor as you love yourself, are the essence of the teachings of Jesus. They have nothing to do with feelings, they are instead a call for responsibility towards your fellow man, without which society and our living together, cannot function. To try to take God out of society and call that the constitutionally commanded separation of state and church is nothing but a demonstration of the total absence of careful thought — and of course of morality.

To follow Jesus, to walk in his footsteps, is not an effort to become holy, an effort probably bound to be a dismal failure at the outset. It means a commitment to be responsible for yourself, for your family, for the people around you, for your nation and for the world, on the basis of the commandments given to us by God and lived and taught by Jesus. Our behavior towards others, whether they are powerful or insignificant, whether one depends on them or vice versa, has to be based on the same Jesus principle. To act like this and especially towards the powerful, which means acting against your lower nature and your craving for security and recognition, is only possible for a person whose security grows from the inside core of his being, which is linked to his creator. Such a person is not dependent on outside forces, but has a value system which is valid for all human beings. A person who wants to accept Jesus' standards of responsibility therefore has to put such a value system into place in his life. That means he has to clean his life from top to bottom and maintain the cleaning process on a daily basis. And this leaves no room for blaming others.

Blaming others ultimately means blaming God, because in the same way I blame others, others blame me or my nation or my class or my color. Nobody normally accepts blame from others, but instead shifts the blame to somebody else, to circumstances, environment, history, social conditions or whatever. The "buck finally stops" at God, since there is nobody whom he could or would "pass the buck." Blaming God means hating God. A Marxist by logic therefore is a God-hater, even though he may not call himself such, and it is complete nonsense that Marxism and Christianity have a common concern for the ills of society. Love and hate exclude each other. Christianity and Marxism are incompatible. Since another word for Marxism is Liberalism any liberal politician who goes to church on Sunday with his prayer book or Bible visible to all voters is not a Christian but a hypocrite.

Jesus lived what he preached. He was a human being with the nature of God, whom he called father and not mother as some idiots do nowadays. Marx was an unrepenting, hate filled adulterer, whose confused thinking was the consequence of the immorality he practiced. Not social and economic injustice but immorality gave birth to Marxism, the injustice only provided the frame and the reasoning. Those who follow Marx and his concepts do so because of their own immorality, not because they want justice. As a matter of fact most of them want revenge or riches or both. Marx could have had a positive effect on the world if somebody would have helped him to call a spade a spade, and to change.

The moral battle for others is the essence of a Christian life, not just the proclamation of good and right arguments. A person who does not fight a moral battle is not a Christian, whatever he calls himself and whatever his denomination may be.

CHAPTER 3

TURNING TO GOD

Cleansing one's life and turning to God is really the same thing, because dealing with the sin which separates us from Him is what God wants everybody to do. It is a conscious act of the free will. How do I cleanse my life? First of all I have to convince myself that my life needs cleansing. That is the most difficult part of the whole process. Christians normally defend their righteousness ferociously: "After all, I have been going to Church all my life and look at all the good I have been doing!" God very often tries to pull us softly in His direction, but most of us are either too busy with what we are doing or we consider the direction too uncomfortable.

Those, then, who think that they are all right have nothing to fear from a thorough investigation of self, It is like an audit which I conduct on myself on God's behalf after having done the routine bookkeeping. But perhaps I use terms and references in my accounting which do not fully reflect reality, as, for instance, somebody in his business might call something an expense and deduct it from income although in reality it is private pleasure and not a legitimate business cost at all. After applying such a procedure for a while one does not notice any more that one's terms are no longer objective reality, but instead are created by oneself for one's own convenience.

31

We do the same in our private lives, and you will be surprised at how many misrepresentations you will discover once you take an honest look at your terms. A "spade is a spade" and a sin is a sin and not an excusable error committed in good faith. Most of us compare our own good intentions with the bad deeds of others instead of looking at people and things the other way around. That is why we think we are so good. After I escaped from a prisoner of war camp in Yugoslavia in October, 1945, I managed to get into Hungary and was walking at night in the direction of the Austrian border. Hungary was occupied by the Red Army. Most Hungarians, though, had been on our side and hid me during the day. One morning I was resting in the stall of a small farm run by two elderly women who had fed me earlier. They suddenly came rushing in and announced that Soviet soldiers were on their way to pick me up. Somebody had alerted the Soviets. I took off across the fields like lightning and reached a nearby copse of trees. I could then observe the soldiers with a dog searching the farm. My foot prints leading to the trees could easily be seen in the freshly-plowed field which I had crossed. Why they did not find me, since I was so close by, remains a mystery.

After a tense day in the woods, I left as soon as it turned dark. But first I returned to the farm to obtain food from the women. They were shaking with fear and certainly contemplating the revenge of the Soviets I would bring down on them. They begged me to leave the vicinity as quickly as possible. Instead I made myself comfortable and requested food. I really blackmailed them. Hastily they gave me what they could find. In no great hurry and greatly satisfied, I continued my escape. I am really a great expert in surviving, I said proudly to myself.

When the Red Army pushed into Eastern Europe at the end of World War II, my father was deported and perished in a Soviet concentration camp. My elder brother, Asche, was killed in action in Russia. The rest of our family, my mother, my sister, my younger brother and I, assembled as refugees in West

Germany with no possessions whatsoever. We blamed the tragedy of our family and of our nation on the Nazis and on the British and found nothing wrong with hating them. We were assigned a small three room apartment in the house of a liquor factory worker. Our landlord, Mr. Kochbeck, had a small farm with one cow.

Our life-style, that of the upper middle class, had been quite different from that of the worker Kochbeck and his family. The atmosphere in the house grew tense very quickly. We lived in the living room, they were used to living in the eat-in kitchen, only using the living room for holidays. They were frustrated that we utilized our space and feared a reduction in the value of the apartment. We had our own electric meter, but the lights in the cellar, staircases, and stall were counted on the owners' meter, and we paid a flat monthly rate. There was only one toilet in the whole house, and that was in the stall, a privy, as we called it. So, in the evening, if you had business there or in the cellar there was no avoiding turning on the light. But the light was always turned out before the return trip. While looking for the switch, we all frequently bumped our heads or shins on something and with that naturally tensions rose.

Our dachshund, as well, was a bone of contention. Our landlord went to the trouble of inserting a small flag everywhere the dog's feces could be seen, to demonstrate the problem. He chased the dog where he could and soon Purzel joined in our antipathy. He barked whenever he saw our landlord, even from a distance. More trouble was caused by our different sleeping habits. We went to bed late and they went to bed early. If we used the sink before going to sleep, the water drained through the pipe at the head of the Kochbeck bedroom, waking the owner from his light sleep. He frequently asked us to wash earlier, but unfortunately we frequently forgot, or did not care.

He, for his part, drove off to work on his clanging motor-cycle each morning at 4:30 am. My mother slept very poorly during those years and would be awake most of the night, not finding sleep until early morning. Sometimes she would just doze off when the motorcycle roared to life just below her window. That ended her poor sleep, and she would start the day with a headache and in a bad mood, bitterness eating at her heart. Soon the deep mutual dislike dominated the house. None, however, called it by it's real name—hate. We *rejected* what we saw as unacceptable behavior by uneducated people. Still, both families were Lutheran Christians and we went to the same church every Sunday. But we never went together. Quite the contrary, we took great care that our paths did not cross. Of course none of our fellow Lutherans in the congregation knew about our relationship, or cared about it.

The Kochbeck family certainly regarded us as arrogant and presumptuous aristocrats, who looked down on them and despised their living habits, and unfortunately this was generally true. We, for the most part, did not see the slightest reason, after everything we had been through, to now come to terms with what to us were the repulsive habits of our lower class landlord. We believed we had a right to our life style, and we resented the necessity of even being there. The idea of winning over the host family did not even enter our minds.

Earlier I had worked in a nursery specializing in growing cucumbers and tomatoes. At that time our real currency was not measured in money, which was worthless. The value of everything was measured in American cigarettes. As I learned on my first day of work, a cucumber was worth five cigarettes, a pound of tomatoes eight. Once you obtained the cigarettes you could buy other things like coffee, chocolate, etc. Girls could be bought also. I saw some workers hide one or two cucumbers under their jackets when they left at the end of the day. Then I saw a number of men buying the stolen cucumbers from those men outside the nursery, paying with cigarettes. They were so-called Displaced Persons, DPs, former forced laborers mostly from eastern Europe, brought to Germany by the Nazis during the war, who understandably did not want to go back to their countries under communist control. They lived for the time being in camps provided generously by the allied forces. They developed their own form of free market society, as we see today in Russia.

Management checked some workers at random when everybody left the nursery in the evening. Those on whom tomatoes or cucumbers were found were fired instantly. I thought that one or two cucumbers were not worth the risk, but I surveyed the area and, sure enough, I found a hidden path out of the complex. It allowed me to take twenty ot twenty-five cucumbers out at a time. I did this three times a day, at the breakfast and lunch breaks and after work. Since I now was an important source for the DPs, I had them come to my room in the evening. It was in a boarding house directly beside the nursery, where we then conducted our transactions. Within a short time I was rich, at least according to my perceptions. That I was a thief and a disgrace to my family did not enter my mind. I thought that I was justified in getting myself a better deal after having been treated so badly by society and the world. After all, we had been robbed of everything we owned after my father was taken away. Then we landed in a miserable situation, with no future and seemingly insurmountable obstacles. I did, however, feel more and more uneasy after a while and left work at the nursery.

Later I studied economics at the University of Hamburg. My mother's sacrifice and work made it possible. Studies did not really interest me very much, but I didn't know what else to do. The destruction and disgrace of Germany left me floating through life without a purpose. I was more attracted to girls and the regular student beer parties than by learning or work. So I had others do the work for me. In order to graduate, one had to pass six written examinations. I had passed five and there was not one of them in which I had not cheated. But I did not call it cheating. I decided that I was forced to compensate for the unreasonable demands of the professors.

When I came home I let myself be served by my mother and my sister as I had done in the years right after the war. Before we had always had servants. Now, Mother and Sibylle cooked, cleaned the dishes, washed the laundry, cleaned the apartment, fought for the scarce food, and earned the money. As a young man I accepted that as the natural order of things.

I looked the train inspector straight into the eyes and lied. He was looking at my ticket and had asked me when I had bought it. "Yesterday", I answered. In reality I had bought it weeks earlier, eliminated the date with a hammer so that the ticket did not look like being tampered with, and I had travelled every day comfortably in the first class section of the train to the university. The lower class section was overcrowded in fact standing room only. I knew that there were only inspections occasionally and saved a lot of money. The inspector looked at me suspiciously but didn't say anything. He marked the ticket for he could not prove that I had fixed the ticket. I cheerfully bought myself a new ticket and proceeded in the same manner as before, until the next inspection weeks later by a different inspector. I thought that I indeed was very smart.

Several years later came the day of reckoning. I had drifted along, but the lack of direction and purpose in my life made me more miserable every day. No girl, no beach, no beer party, no discussion, not anything I did made me feel better. I shuddered at the future I had ahead of me. And I didn't have a clue about what to do about it. "Why don't you ask God for an answer to your misery," a friend suggested. "That is ridiculous," I answered, "He has no time to bother about the details of my life or about those of the billions of people on this globe. He won't speak to me." I was, of course, mistaken. As I soon discovered, it wasn't that God had not tried to speak to me, I simply had not listened to Him. But first I argued for quite a while with my friend, who listened patiently and continued to suggest that I try for myself. Finally I gave in and asked him how to go about it. "Very simple," he answered, "take some writing paper, sit quietly alone somewhere, listen to your own inner voice and write down, without editing, what comes to your mind. If you want to go systematically about it," he added, "look at your relationship to God's absolute truth, His commandments which for simplification you might summarize as absolute honesty, absolute purity, absolute unselfishness, and absolute love." I began to feel uncomfortable without knowing why. But I proceeded as he suggested, retired to my room, sat down and started to meditate on our conversation. It took plenty of paper.

What does he mean by purity, I wondered. The whore I had slept with came to my mind. Reluctantly I wrote down "whore" since I didn't remember her name. And at that point, like a flash of lightning, I knew what sin was, and that I was nothing but a miserable fake. More of the same came to mind. I wrote it down, and then a dam broke inside of me. I wrote and wrote and wrote. When, exhausted, I finally could think of no more, I had a package of papers in my hand filled with my sins, one uglier than the one before. Being baptized and going to church had not made me a Christian. I wasn't just a miserable fake, I was an arrogant pig, having violated about every command Jesus had given us. At the heart of my misery was a tremendous arrogance. Because of our family's aristocratic tradition of nearly a thousand years I felt that I was better than others. That was why I had treated the Kochbecks, the women in Hungary, and many others like dirt. Disgusted with myself, I took the signet ring with our family's coat-of-arms off my finger and threw it out the window.

When my friend came looking for me he found me in tears. I did not think I could ever look anybody in the eye anymore. I was so ashamed about my life and what I had done. I told him everything and that was not easy. What had made me believe until then that I was a Christian I just can't imagine. I wasn't smart, I was blind, deaf and dumb. My friend told me that Jesus had died for me to cleanse me from all of my sins. That truth stopped being just an intellectual theory for me, because I knew

I could not live on without it. We knelt down together and I gave my life to God.

It took me many weeks to make restitution to all those I had harmed. My mother and my sister Sibylle were stunned when I not only apologized to them, but began doing the dishes. But, when I suggested to my mother that she needed to change, too, she indignantly tried to put me into my place and complained to friends that her son had no respect for her. She realized, of course, that that was not true, that it was her pride which put up a smoke screen of defense. She knew that I loved her and wanted the best for her. So she faced herself as I had done and found her hatred of God. She blamed God for the death of my father, the destruction of her marriage and of our country and for all her sufferings at the core of her being. She saw the sin of her hatred of the Kochbecks, the Nazis and the British, which consumed her, but she could not quite free herself from it. Her head said hatred is wrong, but her heart clung to it.

One day she went down on her knees and prayed for forgiveness and told God that she would not get up until He helped her to accept what had happened to her, and had freed her from that terrible hatred. It took two hours, but God worked a miracle in her. She got up a free and happy woman, who immediately started to occupy herself with the needs of others. My sister found the same experience, and as a result God came into the center of our family and our life together was totally transformed.

Eventually the Kochbecks became our friends. They responded generously and warmly when we apologized to them and told them about ourselves. I became honest with my professors, with the manager of the nursery, the German Railways, and many others. I paid money back for crimes which should have, at various times, landed me in prison. Most of the people I apologized to were so surprised and forgave me. One of the professors, who was close to retirement, told me that in all his years as a university teacher no student ever had confessed cheating to him. I had to repeat only one of the five examinations, the one I knew least about. I worked, for the first time like a dog, and graduated shortly afterwards with surprising good results. But above all, I became a free man. I had nothing to hide any more. Nobody could blackmail me. Jesus had forgiven me. I knew that God loved me. I had found a purpose bigger than myself, and began to experience the excitement of living straight and fighting for others. I could of course not apologize to the Hungarian women; I had to leave that relationship to God. And with regard to my family ring I had tossed, well I went into the garden and recovered it. I realized that there is nothing wrong with being proud of one's heritage and tradition, on the contrary, it is part of us. What is damnable is the arrogance of thinking one is better than his fellow man.

"The flight to the moon did not give me peace inside," stated astronaut Brigadier General Charlie Duke at a Leadership Prayer Breakfast in Colorado Springs. "When I came back from the moon I tried to convert the moon experience into money. Soon we had everything the American dream represents: money, success, fame. Outside I was a Christian, inside I was empty. I was a 'churchian'." Duke realized that he could not serve God and money at the same time.

CHAPTER 4

GOD'S GUIDANCE

God takes an active part in the lives of people. While many are determined to shut Him out because they do not like His moral requirements, others are just too busy or too sure of themselves as to bother about what He might have in store for them. God's interest in us, though, is not based on our merit. I am the perfect proof for that statement. Still today I marvel at the incredible fact that God wanted me to be his own from the beginning, and that he was always there and waiting for me when I went astray, never giving up on me. He always put me back on the right track and made good for my sins, mistakes and misjudgments.

God's guidance shows up in two ways. The first I might call the *unseen hand*. A person might take a certain course of action, considering it to be right, or inspired by God, and suddenly he runs against a wall. Did God lead the Jewish people to the Red Sea in order for them to be stopped there and caught by the Egyptians? Do you think that the parting of the Red Sea, which enabled them to walk through, is a one-time historical event of God's helping hand? It is not. And I am certain that there are innumerable people who have had the experience of inexplicable, miraculous interventions in desperate situations. Some recognize the unseen hand, yet others don't. God very often guides and clears the way for you without being asked to. You may not even notice it. What if He would send an invoice for services rendered?

And then there is His guidance in response to someone asking for it.

The Unseen Hand

In May 1945, 200,000 German soldiers, contrary to the stipulations of the surrender document, were herded in long columns to camps in the interior of Yugoslavia. I was one of them—20 years old. We called it the death march. Dead Croatian and German soldiers lay in the trenches everywhere. Soldiers and civilians were being killed left and right by vengeful partisans. There was scarcely a thing to eat. In the evening I could sometimes only keep going on my hands and knees. We were all prepared to die. For the first time since I was in the war, where I had been a tank gunner, I really expected to die. If they don't shoot me, I thought, I will surely starve. Half of the 200,000 German prisoners of war did not survive the march and the following internment. I am one of the survivors.

Five months later five of us escaped at night from our camp, which was a crime punishable by death. We ran into an army patrol and lost our leader who had the only map. We re-grouped and walked at night following the north star, eating what we could find or dig out of the fields. Before daybreak we hid, mostly in forests, where we remained until dark.

One morning there was no cover to be found and it was long after sunrise that we found some low bushes located beside a crossroad. Until noon, all was fine. Then a man with a dog on a leash came by. The dog barked and pulled the man in our direction. I looked right into his searching eyes through the few branches with which I had covered myself. After a brief hesitation and without taking any action the man left. He did not come back. When the night fell we moved on.

We had to cross the river Drau, the borderline between Croatia, then part of Yugoslavia and Hungary. It was so cold that I considered giving myself up to the partisans, running the risk of being shot, rather than swimming through the river, as we had planned at the outset. Precisely at the point where we reached the Drau we found a boat which was lying under water. Having a sailor among us, that posed no problem, we had it afloat without much delay and started to cross the river. It was a full moon and clear as day. We did not understand why nobody was shooting at us. It turned out that this was not the border, it was only an arm of the Drau. The main bed of the river we reached two nights later.

Again, precisely at the point where we hit the river, which was much broader than the river arm, there was a boat waiting for us, this time tied to a tree and fully equipped with oars. We wasted no time in crossing the border. Nobody shot at us this time either. We then started to ask the Hungarians for help and they fed us. We continued in two groups, to make it a lesser effort for those who gave us shelter and food. Then, there was the escape from the Soviet army patrol who was chasing us.

We still had to cross various borders, beginning with the Hungarian-Austrian border. By the time I got there I was alone. A Hungarian took me to the other side after I had helped him to violate the law, which forbade the Hungarians from slaughtering and eating their own animals. Then I got to the border between the Soviet and British occupation zones, the decisive one, the last obstacle before reaching the free world. I had been dreaming of getting that far, but not really expecting to reach it—and now I was there. A farmer put me up for the night and told me that I had to cross a small bridge the next day, before the guard arrived about one mile from where we were, at dawn. "It is very easy," he said. He assured me I should sleep in peace and he would wake me in time. Very satisfied, I retired to sleep in the stable. When I woke up it was already light. The farmer had forgotten to wake me. The day had just begun and I no longer possessed the equanimity to wait another twenty-four hours. Thus I took off at a run, to still reach the bridge in time. As soon as I had left the village I saw the bridge in the distance. There was no Soviet soldier to be seen. To the left was a solitary farm, behind it a patch of woods. The narrow path wound past both to the bridge. I walked toward it quickly. When I had come within 300 feet of the farm, a Soviet solder suddenly came around the wooded patch toward me. A rifle was slung over his shoulder. My blood seemed to freeze in my veins. I continued on mechanically. But this time I really saw no chance. At the moment I reached for my freedom it seemed lost. All had been for nothing. Just as I was thinking that, the path split and turned left to the farm. Without much thought, I followed it and walked up to the barn door. Having arrived, I knocked, or rather pretended to, since I had no intention of bringing out the inhabitants, whose attitudes were unknown to me. While I was standing there with my back turned toward the Soviet soldier, I expected a great mass to approach and grab me by the neck. I pulled up my shoulders and waited for the inevitable. Nothing happened! Finally I looked around carefully. The soldier had walked on and was already quite far away, and nearing the village. I was on the other side of the bridge in no time.

I think that a person can only really appreciate freedom if he has once lost it. It was a defining moment, but not yet a turning point in my life. By crossing the bridge I had left the Soviet realm of power and had thus escaped forced labor and probably certain death. And as I thought back on the weeks of my escape, they appeared to be like a chain of extraordinary, inexplicable, fortunate occurrences. My path had been cleared as if by magic. My faith at the time was purely theoretical. In fact I had not thought about God at all. Now the idea entered my head that God might well have had a hand in the events and that He might have something in mind for my life. But I soon dismissed that notion and continued to live like a pagan. The turning point in my life came when God, years later, shook me to the roots, showed me who I am, and gave a purpose and meaning to my life far beyond myself. Then I knew for certain that it indeed had been He who had kept me alive, cleared the obstacles and led me to freedom—for a reason!

I could now say that this experience is my proof that God exists, but it is only the beginning of the proof. Some people might argue that such a series of helpful events is just extended luck. David Hume, a British atheist and philosopher of the eighteenth century, and famous for his attacks against miracles reported in the Bible, would probably declare that these personal experiences do not prove anything. He had discarded testimony by the apostles and other eyewitnesses as wild imaginations of ignorant people in underdeveloped countries and concluded, "it appears that no testimony for any kind of miracle has ever amounted to a probability, much less to a proof."[1] For Hume, Christian religion and faith meant believing something which is contrary to reason, custom and experience, implying that it is something for people who don't have much intelligence. He called religion "sick men's dreams."[2] It did obviously not occur to him that what was really sick was his own thinking, because he was talking arrogantly about something which he knew nothing about. The same applies to Bertrand Russel who had the following to say: "I regard (religion) as a disease born of fear and as a source of untold misery to the human race. I cannot, however, deny that it has made some contributions to civilization. It helped in early days to fix the calendar and it caused Egyptian priests to chronicle eclipses with such care that in time they became able to predict them. These two services I am prepared to acknowledge, but I do not know of any others."[3] There is an additional dimension to life and mind which can only be grasped by people who consent to let God clarify His truth about themselves to them, and who search for His guidance on a daily basis. Most of the army of theologians and philosophers are like people who sit in a forest and can't find a tree. They come up with elaborate intellectual constructions, and argue endlessly among themselves, but move in an intellectual cavity without any spiritual link to the themes they talk about so wisely. It can of course be argued rightfully whether, for instance, my encounter with those two boats in the rivers and the other incidents (I only reported the most striking) constitute miracles or not. Naturally the boats did not come down from heaven at night, when nobody could see them transported, by an angel who was ordered by God to put them there. There was a logical, even worldly, reason for them to be in their respective places, and we got there, not on a cloud, but on our feet. The difference between a spiritual and a non-spiritual (only what I can touch) manner of looking at events and the interpretation of what happened (and why) is considerable. It depends on each individual. It, however, is worth remembering that in court proceedings there is what is called proof by circumstantial evidence. Many repetitions of the same general event lead first to probability and then to the establishment of a fact.

To Listen to God

"We have two ears and one mouth. Why don't we listen twice as much as we talk?" I don't remember who coined this phrase, but it is certainly relevant, not only to the proper relation of praying and listening to God but, for many aspects of daily life including marriage. "Blessed are the ears which don`t listen to the voice from outside but to the truth being taught in your inside," said the Augustinian monk, Thomas a Kempis[3]. He said that in the 15th century, long before there were Protestants or Baptists. He pointed out that God, who taught the prophets, never stopped speaking to all people, but encounters nothing but deaf ears and closed hearts. "Shut the door to your sensuality so that you can hear what the Lord, your

God, tells you,[3]" he admonishes. "When man listens, God gives him ideas. And when man chooses to be governed by these ideas, he becomes a new type of man," said Frank N.D. Buchman the founder of Moral Rearmament, 1957.

I normally start my day very early with prayer and reading a passage in the Bible. Then I take a piece of paper and write my thoughts down. There are no bells and no flashing lights. You might call that half-hour a rational planning session. I record what I have to do that day, I evaluate what happened the day before to me or to the country or to other places and people in the world close to my heart or relevant to the ideological struggle. I search my heart to see if I am still in line with God's commandments and whether my short-term activities are integrated properly into my long-term purposes. Did I hurt Dina, my wife? Do I answer the needs of my children? Are there any ungodly desires or resentments hidden in my heart which confuse my thought and action? If I did something wrong, I ask for forgiveness, put it in order and go on. I do not let myself be dragged down by my sinful and difficult human nature, or by whatever difficulties and catastrophes are part of life.

If there is a shred of self-pity, self-righteousness, envy or impurity in me I throw it out, because I know that "you can't live crooked and think straight." Every day brings a new beginning and I may be completely mistaken but I always feel part of eternity, of God's purposes for this world, and understand myself as a part of the battle for truth and the defeat of the lie, in order to enlighten humanity that it may follow God's road, and not the garden path down to self-destruction.

Often God guides one to do things which one doesn't like at all. And very often uncertainty remains as to whether something is God's will or your own. One has to risk, as I had to in many occasions, but overall purpose and absolute moral standards help. For many years I was managing director of an automotive parts company, a supplier to the Volkswagen plant in Puebla, Mexico. My factory was in Mexico City where we

47

lived. When we had to raise our prices, I went to Puebla to negotiate the increase and since we had an inflation which reached an annual rate of 150 percent, I had to make the two-hour trip quite often during the course of a year. Volkswagen had established a rule: all suppliers had to discuss their cost calculations with Volkswagen, in order to justify any increase. A price negotiation between the mighty buyer and the much smaller, sales-hungry supplier normally ended with a lower price increase than was requested. That led to the situation where practically every supplier inflated his costs. That way Volkswagen could cut and the supplier still would get the price he needed.

I did not like the idea that another company, of whatever size or importance, should be able to look into my books, nor have a say in what the right price for my product should be. They are free not to buy from me if my price is too high, I thought. That of course would have been devastating, since they bought about forty percent of my product. On the other hand, I did not want to get into the same habit as the others, and base my relation to my most important client on a lie. "We can not live with the truth! If we do, we go under" the owner of one factory told me. In other words, he like the others, felt that you have to lie in order to succeed.It was therefore no big surprise to me when in my quiet time one morning, I wrote down on my paper, "~~Don't lie and don't cave in.~~" The thought was fully in accordance with my commitment. I knew what I had to do.

Soon I sat opposite the buyer assigned to my company. His assistant was present, too, in a conference room in the Volkswagen plant in Puebla. I pointed out the inflation rate to them and what it meant to the exchange rate with the German mark, since I got my raw material, a special steel, from Germany. All of that was of course known to them, and I finished by saying that therefore, unfortunately, we had to raise our price which from now on would be such-and-such. He smiled and asked, "May I see your price calculations?" I smiled back, as friendly as I could, and answered "No." "You know," he said still friendly, "I cannot grant you an increase, unless I determine myself, on the basis of checking your costs, that the increase you want is warranted." Again I smiled back and said as politely as I could, "You know, why don't you look after the costs of your company, while I look after those of my company. As I stated earlier, my new price is such-and-such."

The buyer looked at me, stunned. Without smiling he realized that I meant business. Then he exploded! He shouted at me in the most vulgar manner, called me an incompetent nobody, who was unable to grasp his generosity in trying to help. He added a number of insults and stormed out of the room, leaving me with his assistant, poor fellow, who did not quite know what to say. Since he did not come back I also left after a while and drove back to Mexico City, feeling very unsure of myself and imagining all sorts of forthcoming disasters.

By the time I got home I had come to the conclusion that attack is the best defense. I fired off a letter to the Volkswagen board of directors, complaining in the strongest possible terms about this employee of theirs. I stated that his insults were unacceptable to me, the owner of an independent company known to them as a reliable supplier with never failing product quality. There were more letters in both directions, telephone calls, and finally my price was confirmed. Nobody ever asked me again for my calculations. When I had to raise my prices it went through without much fuss. But I never abused that trust. That buyer was dismissed some time later on. I do not know whether that had anything to do with this incident, but from that point on I had the respect of the president of Volkswagen and the people I had to deal with in that company. The relations were straightforward and very good.

If it was God, who had told me to stick to my guns that morning in my quiet time, His advice was that of a good businessman. You need not lie to succeed. Truth is better. It takes you further, and you remain true to yourself. And since God is absolute truth, this experience was another sign to me that God exists and guides you if you search for it for Him in all matters.

And what if the President, the members of Congress and of the Supreme Court, to name only a few, would start their day in the silence of their homes, listening to God and asking for His wisdom and guidance on the affairs of the nation and of the world? Would that be dangerous for America? Would it be unconstitutional? John Adams had fought in the front rank of his country's political and ideological struggles, but his fundamental battle was with himself, describes Francis Bradley in his book *The American Proposition.* His early resolve to "conquer (my) natural pride and conceit; subdue every unworthy passion" is recorded in his diary, and it was without doubt this struggle for self-mastery which bred in John Adams a conviction that "public virtue" must be the heart of the Republic. He sometimes doubted if America possessed sufficient of this quality to support a republic, yet he was convinced that it was the duty of a political leader to help shape the character of the people.

CHAPTER 5

GOD AND JOB
SECURITY

When things get tough most of us act like that businessman in Mexico who told me that he had to lie because he could not survive with the truth. For most of us cutting corners is a normal way of life, even if things are not tough. We believe that it is necessary to advance in life. It is not easy to understand that precisely the opposite is true. While one might achieve a better income and be better off materially, at the same time you destroy your own character with the inevitable negative consequences, especially in the family. Children above all need parents who teach them character.

As a businessman, I believe that honesty is financially, by far, more sound than dishonesty. If God is truth what then is the opposite, the lie? Who is the liar who told this Mexican businessman that he needed to follow the lie? Truth and lies do not come from outside, they are like two conflicting voices within yourself. Whom do you follow in the reality of your daily life, the truth or the lie? You may claim to be a Christian, but if you take a closer look at yourself, you may discover that you follow the opposite.

In the 1980s the Department of Justice conducted an investigation of the Hertz car rental company. For seven years

51

the company had billed artificially high repair costs to customers who had been involved in accidents. Forms and signatures were forged, computer programs had been installed which included the inflated costs, two different accounting proceedures were in place, one for internal use, and one for the customers. In total, 13 million dollars flowed illegally into the accounts of Hertz not really a big amount for the size of that company, I would say. Hertz admitted the facts, apologized and paid up. The striking feature for me in this story was the fact that hundreds of employees must have been involved in the scheme. There could have been no doubt in their minds that they were required by their superiors to help Hertz cheat other people. Why did they do it? There is only one possible answer: to keep their jobs.

There is no moral difference between the actions of these Hertz employees and the actions of millions of Germans *(including myself)* who had "no part" in the crimes of the Nazis. But we did not dare, or care, to stand up and be counted. Therewith we made it possible for the Nazis to commit their atrocities.

You cannot be a Christian and a selfseeking bystander at the same time. As a rule, a bystander does not take responsibility for others, because he lacks moral clarity and is cutting corners somewhere. The preoccupation with self and one's own job security which is not the same as fighting with all your strength to secure your family's and your own livelihood leads people to moral compromises. It means not trusting God and his commandments, but turning your back on Him, abandoning His rules, and taking matters into your own crooked hands.

That automatically hurts others and hurts the integrity of the nation. As I am, so is my nation. As a rule, those who do not trust God are not straight morally. The question then is: what comes first, God or job? The honest answer to this question will shed light on another: Who is responsible for the moral decline of America, the Liberals or the Christians?

"What is truth?" Pontius Pilate asked the radical right wing religious fanatic standing before him, who had above all demanded (imagine!) that people should live straight. Pilate was accustomed to presenting things in the way which best served his own interests, and the wishes of his boss, the Roman emperor. He naturally thought that others behaved in the same way. Perhaps he asked the question because he was looking for a philosophical discussion, which such a question normally provokes, without getting the participants any closer to the truth.

Jesus had defined his vocation as bearing witness to truth. "The reason for my birth and the reason for my coming into the world is to witness to the truth. Every man who loves truth recognises my voice."[1] But he did not answer the question posed by the man in whose power he found himself, because that man sought justification and not truth. Pilate was an opportunist, and like all opportunists, closed to truth whose voice he could not hear. He did not need a definition from the mouth of his prisoner, who knew that he could have found the answer to his question within himself — just as all men at all times in history can find the truth within themselves. But Pilate, like generations before and after him, did not want to listen because of the consequences.

Pilate knew that Jesus was innocent. "I have found nothing criminal about him, in spite of all your accusations. And neither has Herod, for he has sent him back to us," he told the leaders of the religious establishment. "Obviously, then, he has done nothing to deserve the death penalty... I shall set him free." [2] But the bishops cried in virtual union demanding that Jesus be crucified. It was not an issue of religion, but of control and power. They hated Jesus with a burning hatred because he had confronted them with the truth about themselves, which they had found intolerable. Instead of repenting and changing their ways, they only wanted to execute this disturbing witness to truth, so that they could go on acting as they had up 'til then.

They skilfully manipulated Pilate, letting him know that he would incur the wrath of the emperor if he would let somebody go who proclaimed himself to be the king of the Jews without authorization. And they manipulated the masses in similar fashion—as is done in today's democracies—so that the people also demanded the death of Jesus. Obviously, the most important factor in the governor's life was the good-will of the emperor, to whom he owed his post, and who had the power to remove him from this pleasant job and easy life. Perhaps Pilate might even lose his head. And so Pilate did not follow the voice of truth within him, which told him that the prisoner was innocent. He did not release him, as he knew he should, but obeyed the deceitful voice also within him, which promised him material security, power and prestige. And so Pilate handed over to the executioners the man he knew to be innocent. His own existence was more important to him than justice. The fact that he went on to wash his hands of this affair doesn't make a great deal of difference to the betrayal of his own truth.

God has made us to his image and has linked each one of us to his truth. Whoever today, or at any time, violates his or her own truth like Pilate or that Mexican businessman or I so many times, crucifies Jesus again and over again. It means also to disconnect one's link to the power of God. In the terms of the electricity comparison at the beginning of the book—you move the switch in the wrong direction and turn off the light. Since Pilate's treatment of the "Jesus affair" was most likely his normal way of doing things, and of treating people, you might define his way of life as living in the dark.

The coward Peter, contrary to his promise, lied three times to save his neck. His sinful human nature was stronger than his good intentions. But Peter faced the truth about himself. The forgiven St. Peter became a force for truth and a founder of Christian civilization. Each one of us can be a witness and a force for truth. It is not the words you utter, but the life you lead, which must be reflected in the society of which you are a part.

CHAPTER 6

GOD AND SOCIETY

Society is you and me. According to how people who live together are organized, we define societies as democratic, authoritarian, or totalitarian. They are unfree or free, with many forms in between. We pride ourselves with living in a "free and democratic" society. Certainly, on a relative basis, America is still a paradise compared with all other countries. But I do not think the term "free" still applies. Partially free is more to the point.

The Soviet Union consisted mostly of ruthless bureaucrats, who through the state owned and controlled everything, and gave something of the earnings from production back to the people so that they could survive and keep working. In the Western European socialist countries, including Germany under Helmut Kohl and the not-too-conservative Christian Democratic Party, people, not the state, own their businesses, houses etc. But they have to give a major portion of what they earn to the government, which then distributes this money on a national and international level to its fellow bureaucratic establishments.

Financial institutions control, by now, a considerable part of the economy, and together with the rest of the establishment have a firm grip on all aspects of life. The average German taxpayer pays 55 percent direct taxes. To that, indirect taxes have to be added: 16 percent sales tax on everything you buy, $3 on each gallon of gasoline, beer and tobacco taxes, car taxes, property and inheritance taxes and even a 2 percent tax on your assets. In whatever direction you move, dead or alive, you pay taxes. The government owns you. It is not the other way around, as it should be.

To understand your own society, and what it is built upon, it is necessary to understand the nature of a totalitarian society. I was seven years old when the Nazis took over in Germany and I was twenty when that nightmare was finally over. I had lost my father, my elder brother, our home, and the respect for myself and my own country in the process. I remember vividly the efforts of the Nazis, especially in schools and in the Nazi youth organizations, to riducule and abolish God and Christian values. When we went to church on Sunday morning there were, in the last years of the regime, always two Gestapo men at the entrance to take the names of those going in. Because Nazi philosophy and praxis was immoral and included the totalitarian bid for submission of every individual in their realm of power, they could not tolerate Christian absolute morality and Christian symbols reminding people of it. It was an obstacle to their total control. Hitler tried, for instance, to make it illegal for a crucifix to be exhibited in any government office, court house or school in conservative Catholic Bavaria. He failed. In September 1995 the German Constitutional Court ruled it to be unconstitutional to put up crucifixes in government buildings. This of course is not the end of the matter because the Bavarians are not going to take this lying down.

But still, going back to Nazi barbarism by goverments and courts around the world is nowadays called democratic progress and sensibility to human rights. These constitutional judges of today have the same lie at the heart of their rulings as had Hitler: that there is no God. They will find out for themselves one day. But the damage they do in the meanwhile is considerable. I call anybody who walks in the footsteps of Hitler a Nazi.

Communism acts precisely in the same Nazi way for precisely the same reasons. There is no significant difference in the totalitarian nature of the two systems. Only their reasoning differs. In both systems God and his moral absolutes as a basis for social behavior where pushed into a religious corner; you were allowed to sing hymns at home or in church but not in public places. Nazis are against that. Communists are against it, too. God's commandments were replaced by the concepts of the respective totalitarian rulers. The Russian Orthodox Church, for instance, was not allowed to take issue with the state or society, and church leaders had to present their teachings in accordance with communist philosophy which means trying to present fire as water.

We had precisely the same situation in Nazi Germany. A bishop by the name of Mueller was the head of the so-called "German Christians." They subordinated Christian teachings to the politically correct Nazi requirements, by which Christian teachings ceased to be Christian, and only sounded like it, because they used the same language. Nazi government action was disguised by clever words but was based on hatred, class warfare, envy, revenge, and racism.

What then is a communist, a marxist-leninist? Let's start with what he is not. He is not an economist who believes in state-owned centrally-controlled economies. The belief that capitalism has defeated communism is about the dumbest thing one could think of. The idea of ownership of the means of production by the people was indeed a theoretical concept in the framework of a social and economic philosophy in the twisted mind of Karl Marx. But it became, in final analysis, in the socialist states an instrument for the enrichment of the *nomenclatura* (the communist leaders' 'in-group') and their control of the people.

Since Western democracies under the Kohls and Clintons and their predecessors have established tax and regulating systems which lead to a similar (but more subtle) control of their subjects, under similar pious pretexts, combined with the moral perversions being pushed on society in the cultural and educational fields, there is no more need for a Stalinist system of control, especially since the economic inefficiency became obvious, even for the Soviet leaders. The thrust now is to control the national and international institutions and set the global agenda from there. To read an analysis of the top echelon of the United Nations and their background and philosophies, for instance, of the functionaries who design programs then to be sneaked into national legislation, would be a shock to the naive and harmless Christian citizen. Alexis Toqueville described already in 1835 this new form of despotism first of all as centralist and bureaucratic which "penetrates the whole of society with a red of complicated, detailed and uniform small rules." It breaks the will of the individual not with physical violence "but it softens, extinguishes, deadens and finally brings down a nation to such extent that what is left is nothing but a herd of fearful and industrious animals whose shepherd is the government."[1]

A communist, like a Nazi, is as selfish as can be. He is a person who serves the interests of his own power and that of his comrades. He has no regard for moral values, opinions or rights of others. He hides his overriding purpose behind social phrases, using the mistakes and weaknesses of others to cover up what he is really after, and making his immoral acts appear to be justified reaction to their misdeeds and injustice in general. He is godless, an envidious and hatefilled individual. Marxism-Leninism is a technique for ruthless assumption of power, and of keeping it by whatever means may be necessary. Not only murder, but character assassination of opponents also plays an important part. Truth is distorted, appetites for the properties of others are stimulated, resentments are nurtured.

Social structures, institutional reasoning and the legal framework are corrupted, and based on the perverted views resulting
from the lack of moral discipline and character of the gods of
socialist materialism. The immorality of the leaders permeats
all sections of society. "Lenin, Stalin, Mao," summarizes South
African journalist Aida Parker (and I add Hitler to the list), "all
were paranoid masters of duplicity, given to extraordinary rages
and cruelty... All bestialised and pauperised the people they led.
Each and every one was responsible for the death of millions."[2]
Lenin, bare of any humanity, was deranged and psychopathic,
who by the time of his death in January 1924 was a complete
wreck and unable to think or speak. Mao Tse-tung was a
pathological womanizer who used his position of supreme
political power over many years to seduce and discard hundreds
of young women indulging for hours at a time in pornographic
literature. The atheism of these men, like that of any atheist, has
nothing to do with philosophy or economy, it is the result of
plain immorality. The societies they created are a demonstra-
tions of chaotic and inefficient godlessness.

"Precisely because any religious concept of a God, even a
superficial reference to a God, is an inexpressible horror which
is practiced with particular tolerance and often even with good
will by the democratic bourgeoisie, it is for that self-same
reason the most dangerous abhorrence and an abominable
pestilence...the class struggle can never succeed until the myth
of God is removed from the mind of man."[3] So said Vladimir
Ilyich Lenin, founder of the first communist state. Joseph
Goebbels, Hitler's propaganda minister and world master of
the big lie said about himself, "I am really a German communist."[4] His and his gang's morality was no different from the
men just described. If they had stayed longer in power, Nazi
society would have been no different from Soviet society.

It is true that the Soviet Union does not exist as such any
more but it is also true that all eleven subsequent republics are
governed by the same communist functionaries with "former"

communists having majorities in nearly every parliament. They hold now eleven seats in the United Nations instead of three and the Western hero, Michael Gorbachev, has always said that he continues to be a Marxist-Leninist.

Western ignorants pay no attention to this, and I hope at least now you know better what it means. The totalitarian systems of the Nazis and the communists are nothing more than an organized lie. Legislation, the administration of justice, foreign policy, the reasons for all and every institution, the relations between people—everything is based on a lie.

Everybody lies, some to maintain their power, others to survive. "Don't lie! Don't participate in the lie! Don't support the lie!," said Alexander Solzhenitsyn to his compatriots during the years of Soviet power.[5] "The most important part of our freedom, inner freedom, is always subject to our will. If we surrender it to corruption, we do not deserve to be called human. But let us note that (if) the absolutely essential task is not political liberation, but the liberation of our souls from participation in the lie forced upon us. " To live a "life in truth," explained Vaclac Havel later president of Czechoslovakia, at the same time "is a moral act,which everybody can perform."[6] If you lie, on a regular or even an occasional basis, you will not see reality. You will believe that we have overcome communism. If that is what you think, then it is because you are a liar, and if you are not aware of it, which is quite possible, you had better conduct a thorough investigation of your life.

If you love your country, clean out the lies. *US News & World Report* headlined its 23 February 1988 edition "A Nation of Liars?" and described the alarming breakdown of basic honesty in America. The lead article referred to the estimate, by a congressional subcommittee, that roughly one in three Americans gainfully employed had falsified the documents on the basis of which they were recruited. Robert Nisbet of Columbia University pointed out in the article that "the number of certain misdemeanors in the universities has risen—

falsifications and inaccurate research claims are on the increase
. . . the whole fabric of society is breaking apart and more and
more lies are being told." "To the extent family life is disinte-
grating, kids are not being taught values about lying, cheating
and stealing," explained the president of Notre Dame University, Theodore Hesburgh. Now we are seven years further
down the drain.

Also at that time, long before the Clinton administration,
the journalist, Lars Eric Nelson, wrote under a Washington
byline: "Of course a number of lies must be expected of every
government. It is impossible to conduct diplomacy or guarantee national security without deception."[7] Really? He goes on
to list eighteen lies which were proved as such by comparing the
statements of the various participants at the beginning of the
Iran arms affair. A great many lies were added later on and if,
applying Nelson's theory, the number of lies is extrapolated to
the number of governments in the world we arrive at astro-
nomic numbers of lies pronounced at government level each
year. It is thus no wonder that problems can no longer be solved
but instead are passed on from one liar to another. Why do they
get away with it? You answer that question. But the result is
total blindness toward reality in this world.

The definition of the "Cold War" has not really been
eliminated yet as a fake. It was allegedly waged between the
Soviet Union and its allies on the one side, and the United
States of America and her allies on the other side. But what we
had then, and have now, is a confrontation of two fundamen-
tally different value systems. On the one side is the rejection of
God, with the consequence of despising and disregarding
human beings whose value is determined solely by their function in society. The organized expression of this concept on the
political level is the totalitarian communist and also the Nazi
state. On the economic level, it is the socialist state-controlled
economy. On the educational level it is the institutionalized
attempt to corrupt children by alienating them from God and

Christian morality. In the totalitarian, or nearly totalitarian, society good-sounding reasons are meant to hide the fact that children are being taught immorality and disrespect, even hatred, of those who think differently. Parents are totally being pushed out of the education process.

On the other side, is the belief that man is made in the image of God and therefore has an intrinsic value independent of function. The political expression of this concept is democracy. Everybody can participate in electing his government and participate in the decision process. There, the right of minorities and of the weak are protected. On the economic level this concept led to the free market economy. Education in America was designed especially to teach both intellectual knowledge and individual responsibility. That leads surely to respect for your fellow human beings. On the one side everything is relative, and, at least on the level of the political leadership, lying, cheating and murder is permitted for the sake of power. The basis of the other side consists of absolute moral standards and power being subject to God.

Therefore, anticommunism is the wrong approach to deal with the evil of communism. A power-hungry anticommunist is part of the same problem. Anticommunism is also like the shadow of a tree, one is always dependent on what one is against, it is sterile. The evil has to be attacked of which communism is but a part. The moral relativity, the lie, has to be overcome with absolute moral standards, with the truth. Each person is linked through his action with a universal principle: the principle of the lie or the principle of the truth.

In conclusion, the organization of society on both sides is but the consequence of the value system adhered to. Communist leaders, like Gorbachev, Yelsin, Deng and the others want to reap the fruits of our freedom without abandoning their godless-base philosophy. The question for each American and Western democrat is: On what side of the battleline do you stand? To think that he or she is okay because one is citizen of a democratic country and on the winning side in the "Cold War" is an illusion. America and the West are abandoning— on the personal and the institutional level— the inherited value system. America has disregarded the fundamental Christian convictions of its founding fathers which provided the basis on which unparalleled economic progress was achieved, and we dare not adopt the relativity of the other side.

And that belies the thesis that freedom and democracy are advancing victoriously across the globe. America is in an advanced stage of totalitarian takeover, setting the stage for the rest of the world. The Republican victory in the November 1994 elections and their effort to dismantle big government will not by itself change the downward trend of American society, unless there is a moral and spiritual national rebirth and the nation returns to God. Big government and high taxes are only the consequence of moral decay, the moral decay has to be attacked, not just the symptoms. There is no Republican revolution yet, only a correction which will have no lasting effect if Republicans misread the situation and adopt a "big tent" platform. "Big tent" stands for moral ambiguity. Howard Phillips and his Taxpayers Party, as well as others inside and outside the Republican and also the Democratic Parties, stand ready in the wings to return America to its biblical foundations.

But the change of command in Washington reflects the underlying moral grassroots strength in America, which I cannot find in Germany. America, from the time of its birth as a nation, has been a very special society with a culture based on freedom. It still has the power and possibility to lead the world either way: to freedon or to slavery. If by definition a communist-socialist society is godless, the question is whether American society is based on the trust in God, as it says on the dollar bill, and on obedience to Him. And if not, what has to be done about it? In other words, the definition of what substance a given society has and what its future is, depends on its relationship to God. All other attempts to define the nature of a society are misleading and shortlived. The German sociologist and economist Max Weber, describing the development of Western society, said at the beginning of this century: "And then for the individuals in whom this cultural development culminates the following description may be true: specialists without spirit, hedonists without a heart and these people, who are nothing, imagine that they have attained a degree of human development which has never been known in the past." He explains that the process of destruction of ethics in our society leads inevitably to the monstrous type of person he describes unless "at the end of this terrible development, totally new prophets appear or old thoughts and ideals are reborn with renewed strength."[8]

The quality of human society is determined by the quality of life of people who together constitute that society. Quality of life is not an economic parameter but is determined by the content each individual gives to his life and by the goals and objectives he sets for himself. The more men live for their own pleasure and see work only as a means to attain that end, the lower will be the quality of the society constituted by such people. Obviously, the more people show the quality that we see in America's founding fathers, the more valuable will be a society composed of such people.

There are abundant statistics about the consequences of the moral decline in America. A mushrooming national debt surpassing five trillion, break-up of families with divorces becoming a routine affair, millions of children without fathers, rising drug addictions, sexual permissiveness, AIDS, teenage pregnancies, and explosions of violence, lead to America's moral decay. Add to that, rampant dishonesty in elections, government declarations and procedures, in financial institutions and universities, and above all in the reporting of the mainstream media. The following two issues will highlight the present state of affairs.

Homosexuals and lesbians have become an aggressive political force and as such a danger to democracy. There are about five million members of the gay and lesbian society in America. They are well funded and important as consumers and voters. A homosexual was not born as such, but is a weak person who has given in to his lower nature. He has explained to himself that what is evil inside of him in reality is not evil but a normal, and just different, expression of humanity to which he is entitled. "God has made me different," so goes the argument, "I can do nothing about it." This is simply a lie. A homosexual follows his preference, he makes a choice and consciously does what is evil. The political success of the gay lobby is partially due to the fact that sexual permissiveness is part of today's American culture Once it has become an acceptable lifestyle, the question whether you practice unrestricted sex with a partner of the other sex or of the same sex is a secondary issue.

There is more to this than meets the eye. Homosexuality was at the heart of Nazism. A core of Nazi leaders were homosexuals. According to Samuel Igra, a British author with many years in Germany, who gives details in his book *Germany's National Vice*, Hitler, in his early days, was a male prostitute. This would help to explain, how a painter with such low social status, as Hitler, had easy access to the top German society at the beginning of his political career.

There were several other known homosexuals among the top Nazi-leaders. One was Ernst Roehm, leader of the paramilitary SA, who gave Hitler his first job in Munich. Another was Baldur von Schirach, the leader of the Hitler Youth. The list is long: Reinhard Heydrich, the second in command at the Gestapo and known as the butcher of Lidice; Julius Streicher, top media-Nazi and Jew hater; several "Gauleiter" regional party leaders; two of Hitler's adjutants, Bruckner and Maurice, who murdered Roehm and scores of others. Igra describes the sexual orgies of some of them and reasons: "... I think it is reasonable, and agrees with the results of scientific research in criminal sociology, to hold that the psychological forces that let loose the sadistic orgies of the concentration camps, the mass murders in Germany before the war began at all, and the subsequent atrocities in the occupied countries, may be attributed mainly to one source and that this moral perversion which was rampant among Nazi leaders and which had its typical embodiment in Hitler himself. It is surely significant that while Hitler's own sexual abnormalities were of a definitely sadistic kind, the creatures whom he entrusted with administration of power over the people ... were sexual criminals of a similar stamp."[9] It is obvious that nobody can be a practicing homosexual and a Christian at the same time. Absolute purity is as valid for gays as for everybody else. The good news is that they, like I, can change and live straight.

I have a friend, Anthony Falzarano, who is one of thousands of homosexuals across the country who changed their lifestyle and found a new life. He is now the head of the Washington, D. C. based Transformation Christian Ministries, and is happily married with two children. He told me that only two percent of all homosexuals are involved in gay politics. The vast majority are silent, and do not know how to get out of their crippling lifestyle. Anthony's ministry, and numerous others, seek to help homosexuals and connect them with the healing power of God. Exodus International in San Rafael, California, is an umbrella organization for seventy-five ex-gay and lesbian ministries all over the world.

The second major issue is abortion. One unnamed US senator told me in Washington that nothing since the Civil War has divided Americans more than the issue of abortion. He is correct, because we are in a war, but not in one where the battlelines are between countries. Instead, we are in a cultural-ideological war where the battleline is drawn through each society and country without consideration of your citizenship but on the basis of your moral stand, which is determinded by your relationship to God. Your relationship decides on which side you belong. But while you cannot choose your nationality, to take a side in this war, you not only can but, you *must* choose.

But first you have to define abortion. The German Constitutional Court has recently ruled that abortion is wrong, but it stated that women who abort should not be persecuted under criminal law. I, however, would put the doctors who perform the act behind prison bars. There are about 300,000 abortions a year in Germany, about 450,000 in Mexico. There are 1.6 million unborn human beings who are murdered each year in America and this has been going on since 22 January 1973, the day on which Harry Blackmun and his colleagues of the godless majority in the US Supreme Court declared abortion legal.

In the succeeding twenty-three years approximately thirty-six million human lives have been destroyed through abortion. That is six times as many as the number of Jews assassinated in the gas chambers by the Nazis. Hitler's program of euthanasia, the destruction of "inferior" life, was nothing like the mass murder practiced today. According to a survey by the Alan Guttmacher Institute, only 1 percent of abortions have rape or incest as a reason for termination of life. All the others are being performed for convenience in various forms, and, let's not forget, because of the greed of the doctors involved, too.

Here is a definition of what is being aborted every day in America: "Science tells us that at the moment of conception, the zygote is a unique cell, unlike any other in the woman's body. Science tells us that from the genetic information contained in this single cell, the sex, eye color, hair color and a myriad of other items about that person are already determined. Science tells us that the fetus has its own heartbeat at 18 days after conception and its own measurable brain waves at 40 days." If this isn't life, what is?

There are scientific facts that confirm for us that the fetus is life and that it is unique life, distinct from the mother, not part of the woman's body, but merely housed in her prenatal internsive-care unit."

The expression "pro-choice" based on the woman's alleged right to her body, is a deception. Abortion means that an unborn human being will be killed. A woman refuses to face up to the consequences of her own behavior and demands that this refusal be integrated into the structures of society as an accepted pattern. A mother who has her own child killed, contracting a professional killer for a fee, is driven by hatred as an expression of intense selfishness. I see no other explanation than hatred of God and hatred of self. She rejects her own being and her god-given destiny, no failure of any other person can serve as justification. This rejection is at the heart of the matter. It is the substance of the resentment in each and every feminist.

It is a close parallel to the resentment that drives marxists. In this case the hurt was not inflicted by the selfish capitalist but by the inconsiderate male. Hatred can be cured, but first it must be defined as such. I see no moral difference between the communist guards, who caused the death of my father in a Soviet concentration camp in Poland, the Nazi SS men who pushed innocent people into the gas chamber, and a doctor who terminates the life of an unborn human being. I shudder as much when my imagination rests on the beastly inhumanity of that act as I do watching on a television screen what had been done to helpless people in the concentration camps of the totalitarian states. There is though a difference. The majority of Germans in the Nazi era did not know about the gas chambers until after the war. The mass killings in abortion clinics go on in full daylight with the knowledge and help of a major part of the population, Congress, the Supreme Court and the judicial system. America and Western democracies are bringing down upon themselves a terrible judgment, as do those politicians who, in their concern for reelection, refuse to stand up for truth.

I listened to a discussion in which congresswoman Pat Schroeder pleaded with another congressman to respect her pro-choice views as she respects his pro-life stand. That of course is impossible, and that is why the issue of abortion is a defining one. Pat Schroeder, as any human being born or unborn, is entitled to respect, but her view that a woman has a right to abort cannot be respected. It is despicable and that is why the clash is inevitable. No compromise will work, regardless of how much some politicians try because already the attempt to compromise puts a politician on the wrong side of the issue whatever he says. What is true for homosexuals is true for pro-choice persons: because of their moral confusion, as a result of their exclusion of God, they cannot be trusted in anything else because they will be just as confused in all issues. It is not by accident that homosexuals and pro-choice advocates promote each others' agendas. A society which let itself be led by such people is doomed. A person who promotes abortion is very far from Christ, and very close to the morality of Hitler.

The real choice a woman has is to say no to her lust, to say no to a lustful man, and to say yes to Christ. No man and no woman owns his or her body, neither of them can do with it as they please. The body is a temple of the Holy Spirit and the property of God. It is like a passport which one uses for the purposes it is designed for, but which remains the property of the government. And that fact does not depend on democratic approval from anyone. God is not a democrat. He is a dictator.

At the base of the demise of society is the unbridled selfishness of men and women, who put their own demands before anything else and especially before God. They follow their greed and their lust with total disregard for the consequences. The breakup of families is the direct consequence, leaving millions of children never to experience the security of a traditional two-parent home. Is it any wonder that, after growing up without adult role models for selfdiscipline and responsibility, they don't know anything but the "law of the jungle?" Selfishness in society is like a cancer cell in the human body, it is like sand in a machine. It penetrates our laws, our institutions, and our life together and this trend must be changed. Selfishness is not some general, unknown mass weighing on society. Rather, it is the millions of selfish acts commited every day by millions of individual people. There is no other way to cure the problem except by starting the cure with yourself, purging yourself of your individual selfish acts. It is not the other person, it is you. If you point your finger at your neighbor, as the saying goes, there are three more pointing back at you.

Where does it begin? In the family naturally. Marriage, in my opinion, is the finest school for character. In marriage the individual learns not only to live with, but also to love a difficult person. After all, each individual is difficult, some are very difficult. And the closer one is to another person, the more apparent his or her unpleasant characteristics appear. Normally you see them in the other person, but much less clearly, or not at all, in yourself. Difficulties in marriage are nothing unusual; they are normal. The question is what to do about them. I have a lot of disturbing characteristics, many of which I am unaware of. But Dina, my wife of twenty-three years sees them clearly. It takes a loving relationship to deal with this, and to change as is needed. Unfortunately, the alternative is bitter criticism and break-up.

A great many broken marriages reflect the reluctance of people to adapt to others. The divorce figures point to millions of egoists who only want their own way, who walk away if they don't get it, and carry that attitude into one relationship after another. The healthier marriages are, the healthier society as a whole will be. Marriage and the family are part of God's created order, and the search for God's justice begins with a commit-ment to justice for the person who is closest to oneself. The failure to respect this truth has not only personal but also destructive social implications.

Only a very few people make this connection because most people do not understand themselves, much less the nature of society. That understanding is truly necessary for a democracy to function. As a result, and with the help of the godless in the media, the education establishment and Hollywood, they think they can do as they please without consequences because they believe their life concerns only them. "My body" is one battle cry of the selfish. They feel no responsibility for society. And that is true also for politicians who proclaim wonderful programs but are unable to solve our problems because of the life they live. You cannot violate God's laws by cheating on your wife on a regular and unrepenting basis, which is always accompanied by lying, and at the same time think constructively and serve honestly the people who elected them.

Former German chancellor Willy Brandt, who was also president of the Socialist International, is a typical example. His personal secretary (who later turned out to be a Soviet spy), had the job of providing women to his married boss. Such men simply do not know the difference between right and wrong, and they apply that ignorance to national and international affairs. As a rule, socialists have a messy personal life, don't know the difference between "yours" and "mine", and if they are in power they ruin their countries. Count the Nazis in too, because "Nazi" stands for national-socialist, it is the same ilk. Count the liberals in also, because they are marxist-socialists.

When Dina and I married, we promised each other not to pursue our own happiness, but to seek, first and foremost, the happiness and fulfillment of the other person. I have failed to live up to that on innumerable occasions, a fact I am not very proud of. But I have always returned to that basic promise. Love is not sexual pleasure in the first place but a commitment to the other. In reality my marriage begins anew each morning when I put aside my desire to be right and to be understood, and instead try to figure out what might be taking place in Dina's heart. When I do not need to always be right it is much easier

71

for me to see both Dina and myself more clearly and objectively and thus have a more meaningful and honest relationship.

Since Dina and I have two different mother tongues and grew up in different cultures, the possibilities for misunderstandings are probably more numerous than for most. Many times our voices have been raised in anger, followed by injured silence and sometimes tears. But then we have always gone in search of the other, even when we sometimes sought that the gap was unbridgeable. There is nothing in this world like a family which sticks together. It brings true happiness. I simply do not understand how people give up so easily when things get tough, how so many parents leave their children to themselves, or to somebody else, and how they just change partners if they meet somebody who seems more attractive. What can be more exciting than to accompany one's children as they grow up in this world and to share with them the joys as well as the sorrows. You learn how rewarding it is, when you sacrifice your comfort, routine and even savings so they may go forward. It is learning, for parents and children alike, that giving is more satisfying than always receiving. Parents who do not have the respect of their children or children who do not respect their parents are to be pitied, but also they have to be cured. Naturally fathers and mothers who serve their family are much preferred than parents who kill or abandon their children. But if you put your family ahead of God, you will not be able to hold them to their best and give them a rock-solid foundation for their lives. God comes first, family right thereafter which of course applies also to marriage and the place of your spouse.

Our society is covered by a bowl of lies. People are being brainwashed and misled by the media and politicians from morning to evening. The ignorance and dishonesty of the education and media establishment has produced an ignorant generation. This generation does not even know any more the history of its own country nor has a clue about what went and goes on in other parts of the world. I have not lived under the

Nazis in order to accept happily the same thing in the country which used to be the bulwark of freedom. Hatred, class warfare and envy is something totally un-American. And America still is the hope for the rest of the world. But I see now here, what I saw then there. I don't want my American daughter and son to fall victims to a bunch of ruthless and godless liars. All American Christians have to wake up to the reality that their society is composed of people who say they believe in God, but live as they please and don't fight for His commandments to become national policy. Our society has to be changed into a God-centered lighthouse society, where people and their leaders live straight, and that will speak louder than the words of any missionary. True missionary work begins at home with your own government. The bowl of lies has to be destroyed with the hammer of truth.

CHAPTER 7

GOD AND RELIGION

One day my sister called from Mississippi and told us that she had just seen an ad in a newspaper promoting a Christian college in Pensacola. It even had an ice rink. We were searching for a school for our iceskating daughter, Sabrina, where she could study and still advance her iceskating. "Christian and icerink is just right," we felt, and so the four of us visited my sister and went to Pensacola to look at the college. An academic counselor, a young woman, explained to us what the college had to offer to Sabrina, and at the same time tried to convince the rest of us that we should read the Bible. She explained what we would miss if we didn't. I could not get a word in edgewise. I would have told her that I start every day with prayer, Bible reading and searching for God's guidance. Finally, I did manage to ask her how they accomodated the different denominations, for Sabrina is a Roman Catholic. She answered that Sabrina would have to stop going to mass in her church and attend their worship services at the college. It was not an all-denominational Christian college, but a Baptist college, I learned. There was no need for the four of us to discuss the matter, none of us can abide narrow-mindedness; this was not for Sabrina. But since we were there we decided to participate in the guided tour and take a look at the facilities which were very impressive. Then I tried to make friends with the guide, a cleancut and friendly young man. I told him that I regularly listen to Pat Robertson and Jerry Fawell, Baptists like him, and that I admire the battle these two men wage for a Christian America. "What are their names?" he asked. "Pat Robertson and Jerry Fawell" I explained, "they are great people." "I don't know them," he said, "we are Independent Baptists and we always stress that we are special and different from all the others, our founder is . . . (so-and-so)." After that we left as fast as we could.

There are 103 different denominations in Colorado Springs according to the Yellow Pages. They probably reflect very much the national scene. Each one has a special angle, some specific interpretation of a passage in the Bible and a preacher who lives from his parish, a system much more desirable than the German system where you have a church tax collected by the government. That money is distributed to the different churches and goes also to theologians and clergymen who then proceed to "prove" (after studying the matter for decades with Christian taxpayer's money) that Jesus was not the son of God and did not rise from the dead. German reverends have become paid functionaries of the religious section of the government establishment.

Things are even worse in England where the prime minister appoints bishops and the future head of the Church is an unchanged, admitted adulterer. I therefore prefer the American way even though the government has churches on the hook too, threatening to relinquish their tax exempt status. On the other hand, the need of the parish priests or preachers to have a parish which sustains them, so that they can look after their families, pressures them to adjust their message to what the churchgoers want to hear. Nobody really wants the preacher to get at their sins. That's why you don't hear a peep from the pulpits relevant to the raging cultural-ideological war, with the laudable exception of but few. Anybody can tell moving stories, with trembling voice, about what happened two thousand years ago, especially if the listeners can't quite distinguish between fake and reality. John the Baptist, who paved the way for Jesus, was beheaded by an immoral king who was offended by John's public condemnation of his adultery.

Does it not occur to any preacher (except Jerry Falwell) among the 600,000 clergymen to say that any national leader who is a practicing adulterer or a professional liar is a menace to the nation, since he doesn't know the difference between right and wrong, and defies God? Can anybody who defies God and His commandments achieve what is right and good for the nation? If a preacher would point this out, it would probably be coined as political interference in the affairs of the state violating the "separation of church and state" with the consequence of the congregation loosing its fiscal benefits. Can their silence therefore be attributed to the same force which I described earlier regarding job security? Why don't we have a closer look at the moral fundamentals of those who have governed in this century and relate what we find to the present state of affairs? Did you speak up? The slide of any country into moral decadence and away from God is not the blind unfolding of history but the result of the acts of those who lead, and of those led, who should know or have known better but remain(ed) silent. As happened in Germany!

I am a Lutheran and a knight of the Protestant Order of St. John, which has the task of defending the faith. When I married Dina, a South American Roman Catholic, it did not cost me any pain to decide that our children should go to the same church as their mother. So they are also Roman Catholics. We have never discussed doctrine in our family. We listen to protestant preachers together, and go as a family to mass and take communion. Our family would probably have broken up if we had begun arguing about who is right, and whether the pope is infallible, or whether this "is" or "means" the body of Christ. I respect the pope for his moral battle and his courage to stand up to the totalitarian rulers who had power over him.

But I see a lot of things differently now. At the beginning of our marriage, I saw Dina light a candle in front of a picture of Jesus I thought to myself (in protestant indignation) "what superstition!" and began to arm myself with arguments to convince her of how wrong she was, and what she lacked, in order to get to the essentials. I didn't do it, happily, and learned that this was her traditional way to ask God for help in special situations—when any of the family was in trouble. Who am I to judge? Together we have taught our children Christian fundamentals and kept them out of trouble in their teenage years. They live straight lives.

I do not, however, believe in the "Big Tent" philosophy, religious pluralism, a kind of getting everybody together and forgetting our differences. The American theologian John Hicks had such an approach, which I consider to be part of the intellectual fantasies of theologians who can't venture outside their religious framework. On the basis of intellectual concepts, and that is what doctrines are, there will never be unity of religions, which are also a part of normal culture and tradition. Doctrines divide people. But where God leads people in their hearts, to the fundamentals of true religion, there will be unity of spirit and of action. And isn't that what is needed in face of the onslaught of godless materialism?

The Jewish journalist Don Feder put it this way: "Judaism and Christianity are two very distinct religions. But there are core values which lie at the heart of both religions that shape our ethical world view. And this is the basis of Western morality."[1]

I have a close friend in India, who tries from time to time to convince me that his Hindu saint, Sai Baba, is a reincarnation of God and by far more important to humanity than Jesus. The attack on traditional values by godless liberals is the same in India as here, and you don't need to be a Christian to adhere to family values. I keep away from arguing with my friend, which would lead nowhere and which would probably end the friendship. And after all, what do I know? Doesn't the Bible record how God can use even non-Christians for His purposes? Therefore, I stress what we have in common, and try to enlist him on the right side in the global cultural-ideological war.

When we lived in Mexico I once took part in a strategy meeting of the activists of our Catholic parish. The issue was what to do in the face of the enemy attack on Christianity in Central America. It turned out that the enemy was not godless marxism-leninism, as I had thought, but American evangelical missionaries!

Here in America I get a regular evangelical newsletter where the author, a respected and well-informed reverend, blasts away at the pope, whom he sees as part of the international conspiracy to destroy patriotism and true Christianity. Heaven help us! On both sides there are sincere people who do not know how to change people and make them better Christians within their own frameworks. Why not work together in changing the theologists of liberation and eliminating their godless philosphy rampant in the Catholic Church in Latin America and the evangelical televison preachers who make a business out of the Gospel? Then we should follow up in curing adultery which spreads corruption among both Catholic and Baptist Presidents.

A few words need to be said about liberation theology, which is supposed to aim at liberation of poverty. It is, instead, an attempt by a group of hopelessly confused theologians—the Brazilian Franciscan, Frei Betto, the German-Brazilian monk, Leonardo Boff, whom I heard preach over German national television on a Sunday morning, the Peruvian priest, Gustavo Gutierrez, whom I visited in his home in Rimac in Lima, to name only a few—to integrate into a single concept Christianity, the church, social conditions, history and the class struggle. They overlook the fact that Jesus died for all people and not just for the poor. They suscribe to the marxist view that unjust social structures have to be destroyed, so that a new person, liberated from exploitation, can emerge. It is pure marxism in a religious disguise and Christian nonsense. Under the cloak of the black theology of the South African Anglican Bishop Desmond Tutu, the Roman Catholic priest Frank Nolan and others, liberation theology also presents itself as a way of redeeming blacks from white domination. If you go to their churches and listen to their sermons, you are not taught the love of God, but rather the hatred of the rich or the whites.

Liberation theology springs from the "political theology" of the German professor of theology, Johann B. Metz, whom I met during a conference organized by the Goethe Institute for students at Mexico's National University (UNAM). The event offered a number of these theologians a platform on which to attack "American Imperialism." They applauded the virtues of Soviet agents like dead revolutionary hero Che Guevara or the Himmler of Nicaragua, Thomas Borge. I asked Metz if it would not be better to situate the new and selfless man at the start, rather than at the end of the process of social transformation. The comparison which I drew, suggesting that a new society cannot be created with the same violent and selfish people, just as a fresh omlette cannot be made with rotten eggs, and that a rotten egg does not become good in a new frying pan, was probably too simple for these deep-thinking theologians.

Marxist philosophy found its justification in the misery of men at the bottom of the social and economic scale in the emerging industrial society of the nineteenth century. Liberation theology has grown out of the undeniable misery of the poorest inhabitants of the Third World in the twentieth century. Western Christians in their "rich" nations, however, have no answer to the problem. The money which governments send (not knowing better) solves nothing, and normally does not help the poor, but feeds the corruption of the establishment.

The problem of the poor is not automatically the fault of the rich, it is, in the first place, themselves. I lived with Brazilian dock workers in Rio de Janeiro. According to their wives the main problem was not hunger, but the mistresses of their husbands. I also lived in a factory in Avellaneda in Buenos Aires, Argentine. The problem of the workers was not misery, but hatred of the owner of the factory. In Siglo Veinte, a famous tin mine in the high plains of Bolivia, I found the principal problem to be the corruption of the labor leaders, Juan Lechin, a long time Bolivian Vice-President, and Juan Escobar, Secretary-General of the Communist Party of the tin mine, along with whom I, and some of my friends, spent an entire night discussing ideology. Except for Port-aux-Prince in Haiti, I have never seen such dreadful misery as in that mining village. But the workers showed us the vertical shafts in the mine into which those workers, who opposed the terror of their leaders, disappeared. They longed to be liberated from terror, but that important issue is not mentioned in the handbook of liberation theology.

The peasant uprising in Chiapas, Mexico, in 1994 is not really a peasant uprising at all. It centers on the Bishop of San Christobal de las Casas, Samuel Ruiz, a well-known liberation theologist, who foments resentment instead of preaching the Gospel. The leaders of the rebel movement are no peasants, there is a 300-man hard-core group of fighters and a few thousand peasants who are being used. The purpose of the uprising is to destabilize Mexico and it is highly successful.

The poor of this world have the same right to human dignity as others. I live with one foot in the Third World, and I think of those poverty-stricken women in a shanty town at the outskirts of Santiago, Chile, who asked me not to forget them thirty-five years ago. I believe that poverty can be eliminated and that all the situations mentioned above can be put in order in no time—if we in America and in the West put our houses in order and submit to Almighty God. It cannot be done fuelled by resentment and by human manipulation. I sometimes get the impression that the concept of religion, and what Christianity is in America, is still conceived as in the early days. There were small villages, sometimes cities, built around a church where the preacher and his interpretation of the Bible were all there was. There was nobody else. No radio. No television. Everything was geared to the individual soul and related to the small world around him.

In the reality of today, nobody lives in a small world, even in the remotest valley, but religion does! So, those who defy God take over the institutions. What is worse, they take over the international institutions and relations to other countries, too. Can any Christian in his right mind believe that God lets himself be ousted by a bunch of judges? Can he accept that God's commands do not apply neither to them nor to the politicians and the way they go about their political business in leading the nation? And that therefore the affairs of the nation are rightfully not His concern?

What is legal is not necessarily right. It is because Christians retired into the privacy of a comfortable, uncommitted religious framework that the enemies of God could take over. Christianity is stuck in an evangelistic concept which by itself is hardly relevant to the power struggle raging in the world.

"Sea of Faith" is the name of an organization in England which exists to support 200 Episcopalian priests who do not believe in God any more, and who do not know how to earn a living outside of their comfortable church jobs. These priests want help in how to run a parish as an unbeliever. God's purposes are not attended to. Christians in Germany in the 1930s and later went to church, and tried to be better Christians, but the Nazis took over the country, followed by the communists. During the time of the Berlin Wall, German bishops on both sides preached the gospel of how to be a Christian in a socialist society, therewith becoming accomplices in delivering the East-German state to criminal atheists instead of plotting how to get the godless out, and God-guided people in. Religion in America is being practiced like a friendship club. It is a form of worship within a group of like-minded people. It is directed at self, at the soul of the American individual, restricting the Christian message to the spiritual comfort of the individual, leaving aside the cutting edge of Jesus' sword of truth to that individual, the nation, and the world. It is a misrepresentation.

What is only a stepping stone has become the entire toothless package. Christianity is splintered into thousands and thousands of individual devices, but not geared to God's plan for the nation or for the world, because the voice of God cannot penetrate the shell of self of the "good" people. Additionally, the flock has been invaded by the wolves in the sheeps' garment. There is a growing number of church leaders who follow the same path as their collegues in totalitarian societies: they adjust their Christian teachings to satisfy the desires of the surrounding world, thus not only leaving the essentials of the nation to the enemies of God, but also betraying their congregations. A larger percentage of Americans say that they believe in God than nationals in any other country in the world. But most are committed to themselves rather than to God. Religion is being attached to daily life as far as it is convenient. A rationale for what is not convenient is easily found - you give it a good-sounding name and then the wolves justify it from the pulpit.

Americans, like the rest of Western peoples, are unable to perceive God outside of a church framework. God, religion, church : that is the accepted formula. A president is one thing and a bishop, or a preacher, is something else. From a Bishop we expect consolation for our souls, from a president economic growth. Both expectations are misplaced and a sign of our confusion. Where would Moses fit in? Was he a religious or a political leader? It is men who put God into the religious box in order to be able to do as they please. How can a king, the King of kings, not be political? The concept is absurd. God *is* political. And so was Jesus. He had the same religion as his compatriots, and no quarrel with it. He took on the government establishment and its distorted representation. And they killed him.

The concept of segregation of church and state, as practiced in America, is an expression of the confusion of Christians on the one side, and the determined bid for power of the godless, who may sit besides you in the church pew. It is as phony and intellectually poor as it could be, and it does not speak well for the intelligence of the American people to let that be the law of the land. The members of the Supreme Court, like everybody else, are meant to serve God and serve the people who pay their salaries. The concept of the division of church and state, as practiced, is at its minimum a total misrepresentation of the intent of the founding fathers who wrote the Constitution. Those men remembered how Europeans were forced to accept the denominations of their princes, or were persecuted if they refused. The founding fathers wanted to make sure that everyone had the freedom to decide for himself what to believe, and how to worship. No state should have the right to impose some formula upon the people as was the practice in Europe at that time. But they never intended to exclude God from public life, declare Christian morality out of date, or accept any moral perversion as an equal democratic right.

"The longer I live, the more convincing proofs I see that God governs the affairs of men," explained Benjamin Franklin to the delegates of a convention in Philadelphia which was to frame the Constitution of the United States. You had to prove that you were a Christian to qualify for participation.

The liberals, in their efford to oust God by attacking religion and the free expression thereof in government affairs, have reversed the process of freedom and led America back to the restrictions from which the founders of this country escaped hundreds of years ago. What is "politically correct" is the equivalent of the party lines in totalitarian states. Those who define what is "correct" have the brains of a chicken, but consider their ignorance to be the ultimate wisdom. The party line is the substitution of God's law with arbitrary man-made rules. Communism, declared by the communists, their fellow travellers and other ignorant people to be dead, is flourishing in America, and Christians have not yet realized how close it has come to us.

Not so with Pat Robertson, who has mounted, with his Christian Coalition and Legal Center for Law and Justice, a most strategic Christian operation to defend Christian positions—a defensive move—and to get Christians into relevant political action—an offensive move which already had it's effect. It needs to be expanded. Similar strategic efforts are those of James Dobson's *Focus On The Family* waging a moral battle for the foundation of society—the family. Another is David Noebel's effort through his Summit Ministries to enlist students and clarify for them the real issues of today. Also, Bill Mc Cartney and his Promise Keepers hit a national nerve. These men are above denomination, and they are trying to strengthen the moral basis of the country. And there are surely others whom I don't yet know. What is still missing, though, is a Christian agenda for America which propels Christian leaders to united action for what is right for the nation and for the world in God's eyes. In my mind, Moral Rearmament, with an established record of healing hatred, and reconciling opposing factions, should be in the fore-front of such action.

Marxists-Leninists begin their quest for power by aiming at taking control of governments, and in order to achieve their purpose they corrupt the morals of the people, keep them busy with themselves, their pleasures and preoccupations. Purpose comes first. Christians don't have an overriding purpose like that. They don't even think of taking over governments for God... but that is where they should start! They are trying to be better Christians—a noble intent, but a very boring occupation. And there it normally ends. Family values are not enough.

Politicians don't need to hear witness of your noble beliefs, but need to be forced to act by moral absolutes. "Don't lie," for example and then try the other commandments.

What is the substance of religion? It is the commitment of life, career and fortune to God's purposes for this world, at whatever personal cost. George Bush said in his acceptance speech at the Republican National Convention in Houston in August 1992: "As long as we keep a special place in our hearts for God, God will keep a special place for us Americans in His." He could not be more wrong; that is the non-commital nonsense of a politician who wants to set his own agenda. God is not interested in a special place in the heart of any person, He wants the whole heart, the whole person, He wants the whole of America. And nothing else is going to work economically and politically.

Religion without such a commitment, is no match for the forces of evil. There can be no comfortable sitting back and waiting for the coming of Christ. Lenin, in 1912, told a group of Swiss and French, that he did not ask for their weekends, but that he wanted their whole life. He knew what it takes, Hitler knew it and told us so, but it seems Christians have still to learn the lesson. The American religious illness, the comfortable preoccupation with one's own soul and being busy, busy, busy with one's own good and religious works must and can be cured. It must be changed into relevant philosophy and action. God cannot be restricted to our understanding of religion, nor be closeted into any denomination. His power, released when we shed our religious limitations, can and will transform the world. It is not enough to remake the government; our task is to remake the world. At stake is not the individual soul and whether it goes to Heaven or not—as important as that is for any human being—at stake is the soul of humanity.

CHAPTER 8

GOD OR IDOLS

Those who proclaim Jesus Christ to be their Savior, and who go to church on Sunday, better ask themselves whether it is indeed God who guides them. Is it he whom they let control their daily lives between the Sunday services? If it isn't God who guides you, and you don't follow Jesus in this way, then who or what guides you? The honest answer to this question could be a revelation, because we are either guided by God or by idols.

When we speak of idols we often think of other religions, where people worship many different gods of whom they have made statues or paintings. And we think of St. Paul and his addressing the issue when he came to a pagan country. I was shocked when I came to India for the first time and saw intelligent people kneeling in a temple in front of images of an elephant, or of a woman with six arms, representing two different gods. And there were many more. This is the way Christians normally perceive other religions and cultures. Then there appear Western missionaries on the scene to convert the pagans to Jesus Christ our Savior. Most of them, I suppose, are sincere, and they sacrifice for what they believe in, but their outlook is limited. Very subtly we, the Westeners, turn in our own minds into the righteous, because with Jesus Christ we teach the truth and the others, well, they are the pagans who have to be lifted onto our level of religious truth. That creates resentment in the elites, especially in India, who look at their own spirituality, linking the existence of the individual to supranatural forces, and at American and Western materialistic and permissive society. But above all they have not forgotten our other calling card, which in their minds represents clearly the truth about us: gunboats.

The question therefore arises whether we, and missionaries are normally part of us, can effectively deal with their idols when we do not deal with our own idols first. But we don't have idols, say the Christians. We believe in one creator God and they do not. Leaving the question of the trinity aside, which inevitably comes up in any religious discussion, there are two important angles to consider. First we have to look (behind the images of the gods) at the substance of another religion, which in the case of the Hindus we find in their "bible" the *Bhagavad Gita*. Whoever takes the moral teachings contained in the words of Krishna to Arjuna seriously and puts them into practice is getting closer to truth than a Christian who prefers comfort to the application of the teachings of Jesus in the Sermon on the Mount. Whatever society takes the teachings of the one or the other seriously, as the basis of its living together, is the better one. Since Jesus Christ is the truth and the way to the truth, ours should be the outstanding better one. But that is not the case. It is a complete disaster. Why? That brings us to the second and still more important facet: what about our own idol worship? Could it be that we are hypocrites, telling others not to worship idols while doing it ourselves? Of course we are, is my answer, because we are blind to our idols which rule us and which we have not defined. What then is an idol?

An idol is a person or an imaginative person who is not God nor subordinated to him. An idol holds his worshippers to his specific and different laws of obedience. Thus, an idol is a false god, someone who takes on the function of God and gives commands without being God. But an idol does not need to be a person. That which governs us inside and determines our actions is the idol we have erected for ourselves, without calling it so. The priorities we establish for ourselves, the real goals we pursue, not the ones we proclaim, and the means we use to achieve them clarify who is our master, God or an idol.

Most people want to be able to attend to their own lives, their families, their careers. They want to improve their lot in life and those who still care for their children want to give them a chance to do even better. I understand the American dream to be the belief that every one has the chance to become financially well off and with intelligence and hard work, the master of his own fate. There is basically nothing wrong with that concept. Without any doubt, America, the land of unlimited opportunities, has become the world's mightiest power and largest economy. This occured because American leaders were able, from the beginning, to unleash the genius, initiative and commitment of their people. And the American people rightly were proud of their national achievement.

But something has gone wrong. Could it be that the allegiance of the American people has changed and that God has been replaced in the heart of Americans by idols? Money, for instance is a powerful idol. What comes first in your life?

You can find out who or what governs you by looking honestly, and without pretense, at your own motives and objectives. Everybody has objectives he tries to realize. Buying a new car, getting promoted, building a house, taking the family to Florida, establishing one's own business — or whatever. For most people objectives are a purely personal matter and limited to one's own life. They are not embedded into more far reaching goals like serving your country, obeying God or changing society for the better. Very often an individual starts out with a passion to serve his country and ends up fighting only for his career and, worse, doing it by stepping on other people. Most of my friends with whom I set out a long time ago to remake the world have settled for secondary goals, are occupied with good works, or just turn around themselves. For some it is about time to get serious. Motives display the true core of a person, they show who you are, your character and whether you are out just for yourself or for something higher.

Normally people disguise their real motivations, even to themselves, with pleasant sounding words. Many knowingly lie about them. Anyone who is honest with oneself knows how paltry things are on the inside. Of course nobody likes to admit that one is selfish, or greedy, or whatever. Politicians and clergymen have developed special abilities in the art of disguise, but most of us are not one iota better. The discrepancy between what we say and what we are, the dishonesty toward our own reality, has led to convulsions in our society and in the world and cannot be solved by people who are blind toward reality. "Problem-solving" and "peace-making" for politicians the world over is to throw other people's money at problems, normally making the problems even worse. The German Lutheran theologian Helmuth Thielicke related that as a boy he wanted to be a missionary. It was not until much later that he noticed that his real goal was not to convert heathens to Christianity, but to eat bananas—he had imagined that where he would have to go there would be banana trees. He pointed out the gap between the "creatural" and the "spiritual" existence of numerous preachers, when the focus of their lives is not identical with the message they exhort from the pulpit. He defined the objective selfcontradiction between what someone teaches—or says—and what he lives, as hypocrisy. That same definition of course applies to congressmen, parliamentarians and governments around the world, whatever their religious or national background may be. What is deep inside is self, people out for themselves, not for the best of the country or for the people who elected them. Pork, for instance, does not fall into the category of "what is best," because it is also an expression of self. The result is the travesty which is still called democracy.

Someone I know considers himself to be a *good* person. He does not cheat on his wife, nor does he break into other people's houses. The people he deals with in business and private should be grateful to him, he thinks, for all the good he does for them. At the same time he lives in a constant war, first with his superiors, and then with his partners. His family life is a mess and his workers prefer to see him leave than arrive. In reality he is not doing good, but abuses others. He does not call it such, therefore he is unable to see the connection between his behavior and all the unsuccessful relationships around him. What are his motives? It is not complicated. He is absorbed with himself. He has created a reassuring image of himself and tries to turn all interaction with people into confirmation of that image, in order to pursue his real but hidden goal: money. Because that comes first his relationships go bust. He calls intelligent business what in actuality is greed.

Money, per se, is not bad, it is necessary for life. But if it becomes a goal unto itself for a person, a society, or a country, something neutral changes into an idol. Modern man, who regards himself as emancipated and wise, naturally does not erect a golden calf as did Moses' contemporaries. But the principle is the same among the worshippers, then and now.

It is similar with power. Power in itself is neutral, it exists, it is a given, and has to be exercised or submitted to. The only question is how, and for what purpose, power is being exercised. Is it excerised for good or for bad, for oneself, for one's own group, or one's own country, for justice, or man-made schemes, or for God. The saying that power corrupts (a reason for many to stay away from politics) only means that people exercising power get so full of themselves and lustful for their own power, that they abandon moral criteria. They lie and cheat, and make their whims the rule of the day at the expense of others. One does not need to look for Stalin and Hitler to find that principle. Those politicians for whom power is an idol will not recognize the true nature of communism or of

Gorbachev, who has the same idol, but is far more ruthless and intelligent in serving it.

There are other idols: like sex—a very strong one. Or success, career, popularity, fame, peace, democracy, progress, technology, the glory of France, the greatness of Germany, my country "right or wrong," the greatest country on earth, and so on. And to add to the list, all the dictators around the world as well as leaders who would not normally be labeled dictators, and governments which dish out benefits. Also a husband, a boss, a filmstar—every human can be transposed into an idol. Many people are so in love with themselves, that they become their own idol. They think that they are wonderful, always right and are unable to admit mistakes. Naturally they cannot fill the emptiness of their souls—which no idol can. Women very often make their husbands into idols to escape their own moral responsibility. The result is blind obedience, or angry reaction, because there are no husbands with God-like features. The second alternative produces those miserable feminists who are a pain to themselves and to the rest of the world. And of course it works also the other way around, husbands who let their wives run them.

Every person and every nation creates its own idols, very often without even being aware of it. Religion, if it is no more than part of the environment, is no impediment. What is common to false gods is that their worship is always at the expense of others and that it destroys real human communality. The adoration of an idol means suffering for others, including enslavement, destruction, and death. Lack of consideration of others to the level of ruthlessnes, is a characteristic of an idol worshipper.

Having created the idols himself, any person can define his or her own idols and dethrone them. A false god not worshipped any longer ceases to be an idol. This sounds easier than it is. Try it. All you have to do is look at your unadorned goals so as to tear down your substitutes for God. Put Him in their place. That process is called change, a centerpiece of Christian faith. If your idol is sex, ("I can't live without it!") and you change your partners at your pleasure, you simply stop doing it. Since addiction to a pleasant habit is not easy to let go, you need God to be able to do that, and Jesus to be forgiven and free. There is the God-given spouse and the God-given time for sex. The world can only become different when people become different, when they change in the core of their being, when they leave their dirt behind and find a new purpose. The purpose is to change the world. To remake the world.

What is essential, then, is what is at the core of a person, the real focus of a person's life. I know a woman who is always busy, always under pressure of the many things she has to do. She is active in her church, in her children's school. She belongs to various committees, organizes theater performances, invites people to her home, gives to charities—she is a pillar of her community and recognized as somebody you can count on for good works. But in spite of all this she is a bitter and frustrated person. Her activities are nothing but a cover for the emptiness at the heart of her being. Her children have various problems because she can't give them the secret of life. She could be different, though, if she just stopped what she is doing, sat down in silence and looked honestly at what eats her up inside and then changed. Her life would be different, and probably quite satisfactory.

A professor of theology, who has no living faith to pass on to others, can work through the Bible from the beginning to the end and back again. He may quote as many passages as he pleases and teach his students what he knows yet his contribution to truth in this world is nil. His insights and his knowledge remain incomplete, because he himself is in the center of his being, and not God. "I prefer to have a vivid sense of conviction of sin and repentence in my heart than to be able to give a correct definition of both," explains St. Thomas a Kempis,

"Better less knowledge with humility than a richness of knowledge with much selfsatisfaction."[1]

The story of a man with the wrong central focus might help to make clear what I mean. The German Field Marshall Erich von Manstein was an outstanding strategist, perhaps among all German commanders in World War II the most brilliant. He devised the plan that led to the defeat of France within a few weeks in 1940. As so many of his collegues he lived in constant frustration, facing Hitler's military dilletantism and senseless orders. The Sixth Army, which conquered Stalingrad, was part of his army group. The Sixth Army then was encircled by Soviet forces and at the end of 1942 it faced defeat. Defeat could be avoided if the trapped Sixth Army would break out of the Soviet encirclement and reach the German main lines some hundred miles to the West. The commander of the Sixth Army, General Friedrich Paulus, later a Field Marshall himself, pleaded with Manstein to give him the order to break out. Both men knew that they had the military capability to do that, and that not breaking out meant annihilation of the army and death or imprisonment for two hundred and fifty thousand soldiers. But Hitler, who was the Head of State and Supreme Commander of the Armed Forces, had given the order to defend Stalingrad to the last stone and to the last soldier. Manstein said that he would help him if Paulus would decide to break out with his army. Neither of the two men had the guts to disobey Hitler. The Soviets therefore reconquered Stalingrad and the Sixth Army was wiped out.

According to military historians this marked the turning point of the war, leading to the ultimate and total defeat of Germany. Later on Manstein became aware of some of the atrocities committed by Himmler's SS in the occupied territories. The officers who later attempted to kill Hitler on 20 July 1944, but failed, had tried for years to convince Manstein to become part of the conspiracy to get rid of Hitler and save Germany. In the veiled language of that time, even Field

Marshall Rommel let von Manstein know, that he would put himself under his orders "if the situation arose." Manstein even could have had Hitler arrested, when the man visited his field headquarters in the Soviet Union for several days, court martialled him and had him shot by a firing squad on the spot. But Manstein could not bring himself to do anything of the sort. In the military field von Manstein was responsible for extraordinary achievements. In the history of wars he will qualify as an outstanding leader and probably part of what he did and planned will serve as basis for the training general staff officers receive at military academies around the world. But all his brilliance, all his achievements and his "good deeds," served for absolutely nothing. The one thing he should have done, which would have made the decisive difference to his soldiers, Germany and humanity, i.e., stand up to Hitler, he did not do. He was unwilling to break his oath to a criminal who happened to be his Head of State. His idol was "duty," he confined himself to the narrowest interpretation of what used to be a precious virtue in the honor code of a Prussian officer.

Incidentally, it was also the least controversial and morally most comfortable road to take. In his innermost core Erich von Manstein focussed on himself and not God. His value system, with moral absolutes which should have made him realize that one cannot cooperate with evil without becoming part of it, failed him. Beyond allegiance to country, Head of State, constitution or whatever form of human making, there must be a commitment to eternal truth, as Mahatma Gandhi might have expressed it, to Almighty God. Because of the lack of this overriding commitment, millions of people had to die, including most of the six million Jews murdered in the gas chambers by the Nazis. Erich von Manstein, who happened to be a churchgoing "Christian," was instrumental in the destruction of his country, which he thought to serve. Don't think that this issue is a matter of only that time and historic environment or that it does not relate to America. The issue, a government which is not righteous—real or perceived as such—and what to do about it, is foremost in the mind of millions of Americans (and not just of members of the militia!) It is a current and burning issue, and Americans, especially representatives of the government establishment, are as confused about it as Germans were under the Nazis. Within a value system of moral absolutes a government which is not righteous, which makes itself an idol, playing God to the people, is immoral. The difference between an immoral and a totalitarian criminal government is only relative. Democratic elections do not make a government righteous. And if was was true for von Manstein that one could not cooperate with evil without becoming part of it, then what about Franklin Delano Roosevelt and his cooperation with Stalin? Stalin, together with Hitler, started the World War II by invading Poland and wiping it off the map.

The NKVD in the Katyn forest murdered 14,000 Polish officers, the creme of the country's leadership. Later the Soviet army stood by, when in 1944 German forces destroyed the Warsaw Ghetto. The soviets let the Germans finish the job before continuing their offensive. By the time Roosevelt promoted Stalin to the status of an ally, he (together with Lenin of course) had already murderd fifty million of their countrymen—about the same number as all the dead of WW II. Hitler had not even seriously started his killing machine. I consider the attendance of Western leaders at the 50th anniversary victory celebrations in Moscow to be much out of place. It denies the principle of justice to those millions of Europeans who were slaughtered by the Red Army and the NKVD—later to be renamed the KGB. And it was for the principle of justice that the West went to war. Or was it something else?

There is not one person in this world who hasn't had to face the reality of his or her central focus. To avoid it means becoming unreal and ineffective. As a businessman I have to run my business. I have to maintain my family and to provide my chidren with an education. I go places with them and do all the things everybody else has to do who has a job and a family. But my central focus is elsewhere. I am focussed on God's purpose for our global society and I am committed to the remaking of the world. This is the best thing I can do for my children.

There are only two alternatives: Either you search for yourself and erect idols, or you search for God and let yourself be guided by Him. He who searches for himself becomes an idol worshipper and a destroyer. He who obeys the voice of God has the doors to truth opened to him, and he will find justice. Woe be unto the people and the nations who remain on the path of their idols. "Their eyes are closed so that they cannot see, and their hearts have grown hard so that they do not grow wise," [2] the prophet Isaiah says and continues, "thus sayeth the Lord, they who worship idols, who choose their paths, and who, in their heart, find pleasure in these abominations, they will see: I will think up the tortures for them and evil things will come over them in retribution; for I called out and no one answered; I spoke and no one listened. They did what is evil in my eyes, and what I did not like they chose."[3] "I, the Lord, that is my name, I will give my honor to none other and the glory not to the idols."[4]

CHAPTER 9

TAKING THE SINS OF YOUR NATION UPON YOURSELF

Jesus took the sins of the world upon himself and he was free of sin. Wouldn't it be fair for you who are a sinner, and who claims to be a Christian, and who claims Christ to be your Savior, to start doing the same—at least with the sins of your nation? Are there any national sins? Can you define them? If you can't, you are living in a dream world. If you find at least one, try to relate to it yourself.

During the confirmation hearings of the Senate Intelligence Committee for Robert Gates as head of the CIA in September of 1991, Admiral Robert Imman, a former Deputy Director of the CIA, called its intelligence shallow, for it always focussed in the Soviet Union on the Kremlin and military developments. These were considered by the various administrations to be the areas one wanted to know about. "But we made very little effort to find out what happened in the republics," said the admiral, "so we do not understand the political forces at work." The same principle of looking mainly at the top of a given power structure, applies also to the relationships with the rest of the world. The result are surprises when you don't understand the underlying forces.

Almost everybody was surprised when the wall came down, or when the Mexican peso began to tumble in December, 1994, and so on. But something else becomes visible: it is our lack of real interest in the people and situations being observed. Basically we are only interested in how a given situation affects us. As important as that is, it is only one facet but not the whole story. It leads to wrong decisions and very often to disaster. Because the motivation is wrong and unchristian, intelligence and government miss the essential. We do not relate Christianity to political action. If, theoretically, there were no connection between a given country or situation, and what we consider our interests, in other words, if we think that nothing the others do, or could do, has any repercussion on us—as a society we simply would not be interested. This means that our basic interest is ourselves, we are the objective of our efforts, not others, and not the world. The world is in such a mess because of this unrelenting anti-God self-interest, and declared to be national interests.

If selfishness is not only sin, but self-destructive for the individual, can it then be right or intelligent for any government representing those individuals to follow a course dictated by selfishness? The problem is that most Christians don't think in those terms. We send missionaries, caritative help, and even soldiers to other countries after having created or contributed to the mess there. Serious Christians are concerned about how to love their neighbor but they don't know what that would involve for a government. What on the one side is the strength of America, healthy grass-roots in thousands of local communities all over the country is on the other side and at the same time a fundamental weakness: provincialism which is content with self and not interested in the rest of the world. That leaves national and international institutions, manned with liberals and communists (which is about the same thing) to promote their godless and antichristian causes with the money of Christian taxpayers. In my case, when I was young, it was the Nazis. Now it is the communists. That lesson I have taken to heart. But even if there were no organized left the issue of selfishness as basis of policy in dealing with other countries has to be addressed. Christianity as a whole is on the wrong track and has to adjust to the modern world and rethink what I might call it's exclusively missionary concepts. The following story, even though told several hundred years ago, makes the point for Christians and their governments of today.

Francisco Pizarro represented the Spanish crown when he conquered Peru at the beginning of the 16th century. Spain was a part of the Christian West, while Peru was pagan and ruled by the Incas, who believed in the sun as their god. Pizarro defeated the Incan armies principally because of the superior armament of his small force which included horses, unknown to the Incas. Pizarro then invited the king, Atahualpa, and his nobles to dinner to celebrate the peace treaty they had just concluded. They came unarmed. The Christian Pizarro had them all killed with the exception of Atahualpa. He was promised freedom if he would fill a room with gold and jewels. After the Inca had brought his treasures and complied with the stipulation of the agreement, Pizarro accused him of plotting—which is equated to accusing somebody nowadays of being a dictator. Atahualpa was sentenced to death by burning.

Pizarro was accompanied by a priest, his father confessor, who also served the spiritual needs of the whole Spanish party, although I cannot imagine what they might have been. This priest tried to convert Atahualpa to believe in Jesus Christ. He held up the Bible to him and said: "This is the word of God." "I hear nothing", answered the Inca, "Your God is dead. But mine lives," and pointed to his god, the brilliant sun. Atahualpa agreed to be baptized anyway, not because he was interested in God, but because as a Christian he would not be burned. According to his belief, the consequence of burning, contrary to other forms of death, was the destruction of his eternal spirit. So he saved his spirit and was instead strangled by European Christians who proceeded to spread their civilization around the world.

The point of this story is that the priest accepted the godless government's corruption and greed (for money) as an unchangeable fact of life. Instead he interpreted his task as a priest exclusively to save the soul of individuals. Obviously it did not occur to him that his task was to stop his compatriots from killing 6 million Incas—the same number of Jews killed by Hitler. If he would have acted responsibly he would probably have been killed together with Atahualpa, which means that his approach was also the most convenient one. This assured him of acceptance in his society and exempted him from the kind of personal dangers Jesus had brought upon himself. In the priest's mind the relation between God and his government was dealt with on the institutional level. It was not his business.

This Christian mindset, being clergy or lay, still reigns today and has to be changed. Soul saving and attending the spiritual needs of people is the essential foundation for human life and human relations to prosper but without a corresponding commitment to save one's own government from godless acts the foundation is nothing but sand. Western Christian culture prevailed in the clashes with other cultures, but not always. The others have not forgotten and the counterattack is in full swing.

How then do you take upon yourself the sins of your nation, which includes first and foremost the sins of your government toward other nations? First of all you have to define what those sins are. That will not be easy, because the attempt will strike at the national self-righteousness inbedded in you, as in most human beings. It is one thing to attack a president from another party for his misdeeds; it is something else to face up to the international consequences of godless actions of your own government. In the first situation you exclude yourself since you are not from his party and the attack doesn't cost you anything, unless you work for him. In the second situation you have to include yourself, but most people excuse themselves since they are not part of the decision making process. Therefore if you want to get at sin, once you have identified the deeds, you have to look for the causes—this is where *you* come in.

It was easy for me to identify Germany's deeds after the war, when I had to face the issue. The atrocities of the Nazis and their German government were obvious. I didn't need to search far. I had no inclination to include myself, since I was never a Nazi; in fact, I detested them. So when I met people from other European nations, I explained just that to them, adding that I had only done my duty as had millions of other innocent victims of the regime. They did not accept that, and let me know that apparently no German seemed to be responsible for the crimes and the suffering Germany had inflicted on other nations. I was puzzled, even offended and couldn't get a handle on the issue until that day I described at the beginning. God finally caught up with me. It was like a blindfold having been taken from my eyes.

"Could it be that I had something in common with Hitler and his Nazi crowd," I asked myself? After all he had not come from another star to earth and picked Germany where he forcefully grabbed power with the help of a few accomplices and perpetrated his crimes. That would have been a natural catastrophe, so to speak, which we might remember reluctantly but have nothing to do with.

The author Walter Benjamin points at Hitler's "social character," representing "nearly exemplary combination of all the fears, feelings of grievance, and hopes of the time."[1] In other words, Hitler was not an outsider, with evil features, or someone different from the rest. He was, on the contrary, an exponent of the characteristics to be found in millions of people.

What were his characteristic features? Intolerance, vengefulness, lack of generosity, and shallow and naked materialism that only accepted the imperatives of power, arrogant superiority without mercy, disdain instead of compassion.

It may be that fear and resentment were the subliminal emotions controlling his character: fear of not being appreciated, and hatred of those, in fact or perhaps only in his imagination, who withheld this acceptance. Thus he was no patriot, but a little man centered in himself, a complete egoist, with a consuming drive to control others, seeking revenge on the world and literally walking over dead bodies.

I did not walk over dead bodies, but I did walk over other people like the two women in Hungary, like the owners of the cucumbers I stole, like my mother and my sister whom I abused. I was arrogant and considered myself better than other people. Was my egoism acceptable to God, but did he reject the egoism of a Nazi? Nobody needed to tell me, I knew the answer. But what most crucified me was the fact that I was as much a coward as Field Marshall von Manstein. Morally there was no difference, I was no better, only I did not have any possibility to save Germany, which he might have had.

My sins made me a part of the relative morality of the Nazis. I lied and cheated for petty personal reasons; they imposed a political system of lies for political and ideological reasons. It became clear to me that, not only on a personal but also on the national level, I was tied to the immorality of my country's leadership. Their atrocities toward other people and nations affected me.

Are some sins less evil than others? I don't know; it is up to God to make distinctions. What I do know is that evil appears in many forms and it has to be addressed and fought "wholesale," and not selectively according to what suits me at the moment. Each one has to begin with himself, with his sins and those of his nation, even if they seem small. Huge doors swing on small hinges.

It finally dawned on me that there are "good" people, people who wouldn't kill a fly, but who don't stand up either. They live their comfortable lives as first priority but are equally responsible for the results of the actions of the evil-doers. I know that Germany's sins are my sins. I had to take them upon myself and try to make restitution. And restitution is what this is all about—to God and then to men. The first step involves the decision to live differently and to fight for your country. And then you try to heal the wounds your country has inflicted on others. An example follows. A group of friends and I visited our neighboring countries and apologized for the suffering Germany had caused their people. Later I was received twice by the executive director of the Holocaust Memorial Council, Rabbi David Weinstein in Washington, to whom I apologized for the murder of six million Jews. I had not killed any Jew, nor had I known about the gas chambers in the concentration camps until after the war. But I had been indifferent to the persecution of Jews who were turned into second-class citizens, a situation which I certainly had watched. Our Jewish neighbors, and others in our city, first were discriminated against and then were taken away by the Nazis. (I am proud that Rabbi David Weinstein calls me his friend.)

When I was in Bergen, Norway, several years after the war, I heard that the following day was to be a national holiday — Liberation Day. I decided not to show my face. Then I discovered, to my delight, that the Norwegians were celebrating liberation from the Danes a century earlier, not from the Germans! I celebrated with them! During a memorial service in Copenhagen, in contrast, I found myself without preparation confronted by a monument that had been erected to the memory of resistance fighters executed by the SS. Wives, parents, brothers and sisters of the victims were present. I found it painfully difficult to look them in the eye, and asking forgiveness for my country was not any easier. I had not been in Denmark during the war, and on this occasion I was together with an English friend of my age, Brian. We were pretty close friends and knew each other exceedingly well. I knew almost all of his sins, and if we were to compete as to who was the greater sinner, the outcome would have been uncertain. I thought it unjust that I had to carry the burden of others simply because I was German, while he watched me suffer with his head held high. He had the good fortune of having been born on the "right" side.

"Why me," I asked myself bitterly? I had not picked the country of my birth, I thought. Fortunately, this fit passed quickly, mainly because the Danes took me in with great warmth. My English friend, Brian, had his own burden to carry, and in turn was given ample opportunity to contribute to the understanding among people. I introduced him to a Scotsman soon thereafter. As a matter of fact it was a miracle for me to be close friends with a British subject. After the war our philosophy in the family was "to love your neighbor is a Christian duty, to hate the British is a national obligation." An Englishman, Peter Howard, a leader of Moral Rearmament, not only showed me the immorality of hatred but also taught me how dumb it is to hate anybody because of race, color, class or country—or simply because of anything. That made me see the inherent contradiction in my philosophy. He made it easy for my pride and forgave me for my hatred.

I also began to see the lack of vision and definition in the West, to which both victors and defeated belong. Naturally, America, as the leading victorious nation, can be proud of her soldiers. I am grateful to them for getting rid of the Nazis and giving me the opportunity to live a free life. But the victory celebrations of the righteous, without a brand-new vision for humanity arising from the ashes, only demonstrate the self-centeredness of the West and the sterility of Western philosophy. It was the Christian West which tore itself apart twice within half of a century, blaming everybody but themselves. Our churchgoing democrats opened the gates for Soviet hordes and godless communism and still call that liberation and victory fifty years later. Does it not make more sense to stand firm on basic Christian principles and to satisfy the spiritual and the material needs of the rest of the world, instead of slaughtering each other and destroying our means to do so? Want to know where to start? Pick a president in office during the last 60 years whom you dislike most. A republican might choose Bill Clinton, and a democrat may choose Richard Nixon. Write down their characteristics, and then write down your own characteristics. Proceed as I did, and you will be well on the way to understanding. During the debate on whether or not to invade Haiti, there were many sound reasons against the invasion (which I shared), the main one being that no American lives should be put at risk for such a police action. I did not hear one voice stating that it is morally wrong for a mighty country like the United States to threaten the small economic base of a small and impoverished island with an economic embargo, and thus put the lives of people at risk, and dismantle a sovereign foreign government which one doesn't like with the force of arms. To demonstrate the administration's real conviction for democracy, try China, instead of giving them most favored nation status.

You see what I mean. Our passion for democracy obviously depends on the volume of commerce. Operation Haiti had nothing to do with democracy, a leftist crowd in Washington and in the United Nations substituted a bunch of right-wing crooks with a set of left-wing crooks, their ideological brothers-in-arms. And the U.S. Armed Forces were abused. I shudder at the desire of the German government to be a part of this kind of thing.

When I was in South Africa in the autumn of 1994 I asked my friend, the Zulu leader Chief Mangosuthu Buthelezi, what support he and his Inkatha Freedom Party received from the West. "None," he answered. He is a Christian, a democrat and a statesman, head of the largest tribe in South Africa, demonized by the liberal press. The communist-controlled African National Congress, on the other hand, got hundreds of millions of dollars from the American and some European governments. Many American foundations, churches and Christian organizations around the world contributed, too, as did many individuals. But the leading force in installing communism in South Africa was the administration of George Bush, contrary to the ideas of Ronald Reagan. The Clinton government finished the job. Don't believe a word of what the media tells you about the new and liberated South Africa. Americans have been lied to for years. It is of course new, as was Germany after the Nazis took over. Several years later the world perceived Nazi Germany's *true* face. The same will apply to South Africa—and to the surrounding countries I might add. "RICE" is the acronym which stands for: Reconciliation, Integration, Consolidation and Elimination, applied earlier in Zimbabwe. Fears are allayed through an apparent policy of reconciliation, followed by the integration of the revolutionary cadres into all structures of society. Their hold on the power structure is then consolidated and finally all opposition eliminated. South Africa is at the time of this writing in July 1995, entering into phase two of the takeover after ANC and the Communist Party have gained a decisive power base in the security forces.

The power struggle will focus on KwaZulu-Natal. The issue is: an all-powerful central government or a federal structure for South Africa. Mandela, de Klerk and Buthelezi signed a document shortly before the April 1994 election commiting themselves to a federal structure and agreeing to international mediation should there be differences about how to go about it. Once in power, Mandela and the ANC have shown no intention of complying with that agreement. Mandela rejected Buthelezi's requests for mediation. Instead violence erupted in KwaZulu-Natal and Buthelezi is being depicted in the world press as being the cause. The truth of the matter is that he and the Zulu people are being attacked, leaders of the Incatha Freedom Party are being killed one by one, and their independence is threatened. The Zulus, a great warrior nation, are the only obstacles to nation-wide totalitarian rule and they will not submit. The whites are demoralized, divided and leaderless. I see civil war as nearly inevitable. American and Western Christians, Christian businessmen, as a matter of urgency, should get behind Buthelezi and his efforts for a federal constitution.

The aim of the leadership of the Communist Party, mostly white and Indian, controlling the ANC is to make the Republic of South Africa the stepping stone for the rebirth of world communism's power—with money from the West of course. You don't believe it? Most of it you can read in the official publications of the Communist Party of South Africa, accessible to anybody (including Western intelligence services) Those services are supposed to supply information to their governments for decisionmaking. It puzzles me that obvious facts don't seem to have much impact on policy. One doesn't quite know whether he is dealing with incompetent intelligence or incompetent government. It is probably both.

I once asked a friend of mine that very question. At the time he was at the head of German intelligence, the Bundes-Nachrichtendienst. Naturally he hinted at the second alternative. Listening to R. James Woolsey, director of the CIA in the two first years of the Clinton administration, I came to the conclusion that he has a good technical knowledge of who is who, and of what political situations around the world have to be watched. But he has no understanding whatsoever of the underlying forces.

In other words his reports must have dealt with what you see on the surface, with explanations which also refer to surface developments, but not with what causes them. If the government operates on the same basis, the result is manipulative power brokerage, which neglects not only fundamental realities, but also the basic needs of the people involved.

This leads to a third alternative, which I witnessed in South Africa. The deliberate installation of a government opposed to our own philosophy of freedom and democracy for reasons of convenience. This is the opposite of justice, and what I call naked materialism. It is not just a series of mistakes, but defiance of God and a reckless violation of His designs for humanity.

The politically correct West did its very best to destroy the strongest economy in Africa and to produce the same misery, especially in the black population, as in Haiti while sending food and money to the desintegrating rest of the continent. If such a policy is not criminal then it is plain stupid.

How often have I asked myself-- what the reason for such a suicidal foreign policy could be. I came to think that one underlying principle could be the desire to deal rather with big states like the Soviet Union, Yugoslavia, South Africa and so on instead of many smaller ones. It is much easier to control the situation, the nuclear weapons, the strategic minerals, etc. that way—in one's national interest. The moral and ideological substance of a given ruling elite or the well-being of the people at home and in the other countries are of no importance to the planners and their concept. Controllable order is the catchword. That's not much different than totalitarian patterns of thinking. That is why Gorbachev is not recognized for what he is and how he has become such a hero in the West. He might show up again all of a sudden for a bit to become Secretary-General of the United Nations, which is full of his cronies. We see him as the one who opened up the Soviet Union and helped to bring down the Berlin Wall—on the surface—while the underlying reality is the same ruthless bid for world power, only under a new disguise: democracy.

The United Nations is a central focus for that quest, you just need to watch the unending series of "world-conferences" with socialist agendas, attended by non-thinking Western heads of state or their representatives. It was revealing to watch the presidential election campaign in Peru (Spring 1995). The former Secretary-General of the UN, Javier Perez de Quellar, was surrounded by well-known Peruvian communists, who obviously were running his campaign.

At the heart of American and western foreign policy is the wrong concept of "national interest." We are led by people in government whose morals are doubtful, and whose philosophies are inadequate and even contrary to our base philosophy. All Western governments share the same policy principle: arbitrary manipulation of international relations for better business, instead of recognizing that universal justice is in our own best national interest. Universal justice is only possible on the basis of God's moral absolutes. It means treating every state, important or unimportant, the same. It is a policy of principle. There are hundreds of millions of Christians in western countries who vote the arbitrary power broker in, who violate the Christian fundamentals and thus defy God. Following Jesus in the personal sphere and being indifferent to unchristian acts by one's government . . . can that possibly be right? Of course not! And I hold the perhaps heretical view that there are very few followers of Jesus Christ otherwise the world could not be in such a mess. I also believe that neither America nor Europe has a valid foreign policy because there is no worldview and no global concept based on the reality of human nature. They are just talking piously about freedom, human rights and democracy but aiming at national advantages and better business. That is the consequence of millions of voters using their vote for material interest and not principle.

During the lifetime of the Soviet Union, this lack of concept was disguised. One reacted to Soviet movements, as one now reacts to developments in other but mostly unimportant places, and called that foreign policy. For a mighty world power like the United States to get involved in tin pot affairs like Somalia and Haiti as major policy issues, and spend billions of dollars on them (which have to be borrowed for such involvements) is simply ridiculous on the one side and dangerous on the other.

There are enough examples of shortsighted policies for reasons that these dillettant foreign policy manipulators call national interest—but which really is exact opposite. The dumbest of all, I suppose, was the ~~Imperial German government~~ when it sent, at the end of World War I, Vladimir I. Lenin in a sealed train from exile in Switzerland to Russia. They wanted his help in defeating Russia, and they got it. Those responsible for this idiocy claimed at the time to have achieved a great success.

They did not, however, live to see the Red Army enter Berlin less than 30 years later, after the threat of Soviet communism had been an important factor in bringing Hitler to power. They did not see Soviet communism become a world threat, with countries devastated and hundreds of millions of people murdered. The next generation had to pay the price for their wrong concept of national interest.

When I asked R. James Woolsey what he thought of Eduard Shevardnaze, Soviet foreign minister under Gorbachev and now President of Georgia, Woolsey answered that he was aware of dark parts in his past but that he was not qualified to judge his character. What he did know, Woolsey said, was his commendable fight for the independence of Georgia.

There the wrong underlying foreign policy principle appeared on the surface, an existing power structure is being evaluated according to whether it strengthens America's position—in his judgment and in that one of his superiors—or not. If it does according to the criteria applied, stability in this case, the rest is of secondary nature. In the Soviet era Shevardnaze was Georgian minister of interior, KGB chief and Secretary General of the Communist party. He was known for his cruelty and his expertise in refined tortures applied to the inmates of Georgia's prisons.

The first democratically elected president of Georgia after the break-up of the Soviet-Union, Swiad Gamsachurdia, is the son of a famous poet and dissident, who was tortured by

Shevardnaze's KGB henchmen. He had published a documentary about tortures in Georgia's prisons. Swiad was ousted by a military coup, most probably engineered by Shevardnaze, who now proclaims to be a democrat and reborn Christian. I think he is a liar. Those who worship power and lie for it's sake will believe him and his former boss, Michael Gorbachev, to be democratic reformers. A foreign policy based on that view disregarding the character of the leaders involved, and their history, is bound to be disastrous. Those committed to God and truth will see through their charade. But those who look at leaders and situations with the eyes of God are able to architect a viable foreign policy.

E. T. Smith, US Ambassador in Cuba from 1957 to 1959, had pointed out that a real US foreign policy had never existed. Neither he nor other ambassadors had received policy briefings, he said. Smith believed that Fidel Castro had been installed in Cuba by the bureaucrats on the fourth floor of the State Department and declared under oath before a subcommittee of the Senate, "I believe that the policies are determined in the lower echelon, and by the time the higher echelon receives them, policies have already been made, and they have to live by them."

American and western foreign policy toward Romania and Yugoslavia was guided by the same mistaken, self-centered "balance of power" principle. Ceaucescu and Tito were considered assets and commended, because they stood up to Stalin and established a somewhat independent policy. They nearly had the status of allies, helping the West in it's policy toward Stalin. The British even decorated Ceaucescu for his merits. He and Tito though were cruel and ruthless slave-drivers, like Saddam Hussein, nearly unmatched in their inhumanity toward their own people whose countries they destroyed. The state department overruled and paid no attention to the US Ambassador in Bucharest, David B. Funderburk, who pointed out the realities and unsuccessfully tried to influence policy towards Romania accordingly. He quit in disgust. The British government anulled the decorations bestowed on Ceaucescu after his execution—the hypocrites. (It is like Pilate washing his hands.) They betrayed the Romanian people for national advantage and so did the rest of the western governments. And you, American Christians, are accountable to God for America's part in this and several other betrayals. Can God's absolutes be installed as the basis for treating other countries? Of course. They can and they must be installed. America, God's own country, the only nation in the world which has a set of ideas, a purpose, as its reason for existence. America has to take the lead.

Again, how to go about it? Start with the following steps:

1. Define the nation's sins.

2. Find these sins in yourself.

3. Deal with the lie.

4. Change and become a new person.

5. Work whole-heartedly in the fight against those sins which rule your country.

6. Enlist others in the battle. That means aiming at change in foreign policy instead of holding the hat for a government hand-out.

7. Provide restitution to those countries which were harmed. This is independent of how wrong any other country might have been.

8. Fight for all other countries in the same way you fight for your own country.

9. Work to change human nature, motives, and aims.

10. Look for character on a personal and a national level. This is the essence of the revolutionary teaching of Jesus Christ.

CHAPTER 10

SET YOUR HEART FIRST ON THE KINGDOM OF GOD

".....and His goodness, and all these things will come to you as a matter of course," continues Jesus in his Sermon on the Mountain.[1] "All these things" he had defined earlier, is, "what you are going to eat or drink, or what you are going to wear."[2] In the framework of a modern economy it comprises all your material needs as a family, purchase orders for a company, commerce treaties for a government—all that leads to income to safeguard personal and national existence, jobs of course included. What Jesus says is simply that the battle for material existence on a personal or national basis must not take first place but is secondary and subordinated to complying with God and the rules of His kingdom. When St. Peter stepped on to the water from his boat he obeyed the instructions of Jesus because he believed that Jesus guaranteed his material existence although it must have seemed impossible to him that he would not sink.

What is a kingdom? It is a territory where a king rules in the way kings did at the times of Jesus: their words were the law. Will you find God's kingdom in heaven after you die? Maybe, maybe not. I at least consider the possibility that you might not get to heaven if you don't find His kingdom here on earth.

Where? Around the corner? What territory are we talking about where God rules? It is simple and easy, not complicated at all. Only theologians and philosophers, who haven't found it, make it complicated. It is the human heart, the core of every human being of whatever religion. "The kingdom of God never comes by looking for signs of it," said Jesus. "Men cannot say, 'Look here it is', or 'there it is', for the kingdom of God is inside you."[3] Are you then being ruled by God in your heart and in your consequent actions? Are your leaders looking there also? Or would that be unconstitutional? Do you want them to be ruled by God? I certainly do, and I am trying to make the issue clear, so that everybody can fight to make it happen. Obviously I do not mean to impose a set of religious rules on government, which would upset the ACLU, myself included. It means to set these people free from the bondage of their lower nature, so that God's spirit can move them. If that doesn't happen soon, then these ignorant people will run us all into the ground. A God-guided government policy will result from people in government who have decided to let themselves be ruled by God. That is, I would say, a very high priority in the national interest.

The proof that God exists, the theme with which we started, is a consequence of connecting with the power of God. How do I connect? I enter His kingdom and let Him rule me, and in the process of obeying I shall know that He is there, even though I don't see Him. There is no other way. After walking on the water, Peter knew what was involved: obedience and risk of life on the one side, or conventional wisdom and the "security" of the boat on the other side. That is the choice, of course in different circumstances, with which every one, sooner or later, is confronted. Peter had his proof of God after he obeyed, and so have I, albeit not such a spectacular one. But the proof which satisfies me will be only my individual proof. People of the ilk of David Hume would not consider that to be scientific proof. Plenty of individual proofs, though, backed up by concrete experiences, and lives that "shine" as we said at the beginning, could already constitute proof by circumstantial evidence. Somebody should start a collection of underpinning stories. The ultimate proof will be when America will shine as a society infecting the rest of the world with truth instead of tearing itself apart and imposing double standard concepts of human rights and democracy on others. We have arrived at the crux of the matter, even though we looked at it already from various angles. I see obedience to the commandment 'set your heart first on His Kingdom' (which gives the theme to this chapter) as the key for the future of the world. It boils down to a choice between what comes first: God or money. It's that simple. Existence normally is linked to money in one form or another. Everyone needs money—but is the pursuit of it your over-riding purpose?

No individual and no nation can serve two masters and the consequence of not serving God before anything else is self-destruction. If America chooses to destroy herself, she will pull down the world into the same abyss. A government which serves money or power will associate with any set of criminals, as long as it sees an advantage for itself.

Check the history of your government. The explanation "we want to draw them into the community of nations" is nothing but a lie. It is like inviting a professional thief to watch over another person's house and belongings (of course not your own) whilst he is away. If a nation through its government serves money, it means that the people who make up that nation as individuals also serve money.

If you want your nation on a God-loving course you have to start with yourself. Begin to serve Him before anything else in the reality of your life. That is a repeated, conscious decision, which connects you with the power of God. That is why, I assume, the doctor, psychiatrist and author Dr. Scott Peck believes that it is probable that the universe as we know it is but a single stepping stone toward the entrance to the Kingdom of God.[4] "God is within us," he explains, "we are part of God all

? cf. I Jn. 5:19; Jn. 17:16; Eph. 2:2; 6:12; II Pet. 3:7, 12-13.

the time.[5] ..we are born that we might become, as a conscious individual, a new life form of God."[6]

I have lived where my mouth is. That, however, does not mean that I was right in what I was doing all of the time. It means that my overall motivation was centered in God. To serve Him, I spent nearly twenty years with Moral Rearmament after leaving the university. I did not receive one cent of salary. Like all my friends from around the world commited to the same cause, I lived by faith and prayer. People gave donations. My earthly possessions consisted of what I could carry in a suitcase. When I realized one day that I had become a functionary of a movement—as honorable as MRA was and is—and that my independent spirit was about to die, I left them and went into business. The adjustment was tremendously difficult, and lasted many years. I was dumb, naive, innocent and ignorant. And I associated myself with the wrong people. I was "taken for many rides." I, on the other hand, ran wild and had given up my commitment to God. I was empty because I had lost my purpose. Then God collected me again. I was, by that time, an independent businessman in Mexico.

At age 46 I received my first salary. That was in Lima, Peru. I received money for work instead of no money for work, as I was used to. There I worked for the international investment company ADELA. In Lima I got married and after three years in Jamaica, where Stefan was born, we landed in Mexico. I then began to earn good money. But even though I was far away from God money did not rule me. I had sworn not to climb the ladder to riches on the backs of other people, especially not of those who worked for me. Thirty people and their families depended on me. "If things go well, and I live well, I want them to live well also," I said to myself. According to Mexican labor law, every worker and employee gets half a month's extra salary as a Christmas bonus. So I announced that our factory would not pay half, but a full month salary extra. It was paid out on December 23. Between Christmas and New Years I had hoped to produce an export order. Nobody turned up for work; they had enough money to have a good time. The following year was good and when Christmas came around I said to myself "they'll have the same bonus, but I'll do it more intelligently." So we paid half the amount before Christmas and the other half on the last day of the year. Everybody came for work after Christmas. But nobody turned up at the beginning of the year, until after the 6th of January. That is the Festival of the Three Kings, an important religious (and public) holiday. For Mexican Catholics it is just as important as Christmas. I was furious. The next year I paid the second half in the middle of January, everybody turned up all the time and this schedule remained in force to everyone's great satisfaction.

According to the law the labor week in Mexico has 48 hours, but in my factory workers worked 45 hours. There was a system of premiums which allowed each one to double his salary. There was a free lunch program; each month everybody got a basket with basic food items; and the company paid 13 percent of a worker's salary into a savings account, matching the same amount paid by the worker. They administered the account, and my share went to them. When in 1988 wages were frozen by the Mexican government, we increased workers' and employees' wages by 30 percent to compensate for the loss of buying power. Constant decline of real wages of ordinary people is a regular feature by all Mexican presidents. These thieves and their cronies fill their own pockets and leave their people with nothing. Last, but not least, I contracted with a doctor, in addition to Mexican Social Security for serious illnesses, and I sometimes financed the construction of houses. Contrary to Richard Gebhardt and his collegues in Congress, who finance their "compassion" with other people's money and not with their own, every cent of this came out of my own pocket. It did not always come easily especially when times were tough. But I stuck to it, encouraged by Dina. We had no labor problems and never a strike. We made a quality product, recognized as such by the Volkswagen plant—everybody always gave it his best whether I was there or not. We had great fun and enjoyed working together. I had established for myself that money was not running my life. My workers and employees knew that I trusted them and counted on their responsibility. Not so with my partner. I had invited my best friend to become a partner in the company at a time when I still did not have an immigration status which would allow me to own industrial property in Mexico. I put all my shares in his name. We had two companies, one which held the land and building, the other was the producing factory. He first stole the land and the building, and then he went after the factory. I managed to aggravate that attempt, but I was walking close to disaster for a long time, having no other resources and living with small children in a country which was not my own. Then I sued him for restitution and he sued me to abandon the premises. As is the legal custom in Mexico, once such a dispute goes to court, the rent is paid into a government account until the case is decided. I gave the money to my lawyer who, as it turned out, put it into his own pocket instead of paying the rent.

One morning while I was not in Mexico a group of people with construction equipment turned up in front of the factory door with a government order to evacuate the building. In Mexico you never know who is responsible for such a development. Normally the most likely cause is corruption—somebody pays a government official to get the desired action. In this case, I believe, it was the negligence of my second lawyer, a legal adviser to the Mexican Congress.

In any case my machines and everything movable was thrown into the street during pouring rain. When I received the news on the telephone a minute before the line was cut, I nearly went into shock. I then agonized that this was the end of our family's material existence. Not so. A friend had room in his industrial complex and my workers under their supervisors worked day and night. They saved everything and had the factory working again in a few weeks. Then I sold the factory and the buyers did not pay up. Again, I nearly went under but after two years' delay they paid most of what they owed me. Does God exist? Of course he does. And to stress the point raised earlier—all of what happened to me and I have only told part of it—was not "natural evil," it was the consequence of my having chosen the wrong people to work with.

Years earlier, I had become aware of more and more cases where what I read in the newspapers and heard in the news could not be true. At least not according to what I knew about it. Slowly I got so mad at the distortions that I felt the urge to do something about it. I remembered Nazi Germany and the Minister of Information and Propaganda, Joseph Goebbels, whose maxim had been "if you tell a lie often enough something will stick." They had poisoned Germany and brainwashed the population. The same was now being done on a global scale, I realized, by the equally godless and immoral left. My promise to God after the war was that I was going to fight so that never again Nazis or similar forces could take over Germany. It did not only apply any more to my country, it applied to the whole world. Their attack, I knew, can only be thwarted in the framework of the global battle. And that is where America and the West are vulnerable because they think in national terms. And that is true in spite of modern internationalism. I had to accept that my battleground is the world.

I started my own crusade for truth, going to most of the controversial trouble-spots around the world, investigating what was going on. That was normally contrary to what was being reported by Associated Press and the other news media. So I went to Chile, Cuba, Nicaragua, South Africa, the Middle East, India, China, Hongkong, the then Soviet Union and up and down Europe, South and North America. All at my own expense.

Instead of saving I invested in investigation and still contributed, in small amounts, to the causes of others. "Crazy and irresponsible" I said to myself more than once. But I did not stop, and even in the middle of the worst of the disasters I kept going. I was sure that somebody had to do it, report and relate it to the individual lives of people wherever they live. My first book, *Cowardice and Appeasement—Doubtful Politics*, was published 1989 in Germany, and later a Spanish edition in Chile.

To set my heart first on the kingdom of God means for me to follow my calling before (but not without!) money. Frank Buchman, founder of Moral Rearmament, had taught me in my early days that where God guides He provides. The fact of my applying that principle, contrary to all conventional wisdom, on a steadfast basis in the framework of a global philosophy and commitment is not, I am sure, just a personal experience of God's power and the righteousness of His commands. They are in our best interests, but are also a demonstration of the only principle for people, nations and their leaders to conduct their affairs. It is the only way society and the world can function harmoniously. And while I am writing this, I am working very hard to establish a new business, so as to be able to finance my family and keep going. Nothing falls from heaven for no reason and, as far as I am concerned, not from government programs either.

Aiming at establishing God's kingdom on earth would mean for Christians to take the prayer "Thy will be done, on earth as it is in heaven" not as a pious phrase, but as a commitment to relevant action. But even those who do not believe in a personal God would understand what is meant, if one would say "establishing universal justice." As much as in a state of law, the same legal yardstick applies rigorously to everybody without favor or discrimination, the same yardstick must be applied in international relations. The same principle to the treatment of China as to that of Haiti. That principle must be absolute and beyond being adjusted to selfish personal and national interests. Out of the application of that principle comes justice and after that peace. One nation must set the standard and the pace. It should be America. It *must* be America.

That implies a new definition for what is the national interest. Is it in the best interest of any nation to allow the law of the jungle to reign anywhere? And should we just go after our business? German national interest is not, as Chancellor Helmuth Kohl hypocritically frames it, "to keep the lines of trade open," by which he actually means appeasing the terrorist regime of Iran and doing business with them without a plan to change them. It is money before righteousness and common sense. Germany, under his leadership, contributes to the establishment of a new, and even more dangerous Iraq. The miserable opportunists in Bonn, in moving ceremonies, praise the moral courage of the German resistance to Hitler. Those men and women stood up in face of totalitarian evil risking life and existence. Many lost both in the process.

German leaders declare piously that they will never again allow this kind of evil to prosper. I think, however, that they are unable to define correctly what the evil is, and they are incapable of acting according to what they say. They reduce evil to antisemitism, and to the extreme political right. To fight those aberrations does not cost them anything. As soon as money and national business is concerned, their own existence takes first precedence and not the example of the dead resistance fighters. "Realpolitik" with other criteria dominates. The same government then establishes diplomatic relations with Communist Beyjing but not with democratic Taipei, bowing to the same totalitarian evil they just so piously decried. Obviously not because it is right but it brings more money. Business for oneself is more important than what is right for the others—another way to describe how to exclude oneself from entry into the Kingdom of God.

The continental Chinese market is bigger than the island of one of the co-founders of the United Nations, the Republic of China on Formosa. "If we don't do it, the others will,

123

therefore we better," so goes the argument. Who are the others? Western, nominally Christian nations, are all out to grab a piece of the pie. Who thus determines Western foreign policy? Totalitarian China, which pits one against the other, also blackmails all of them with their greed for business. I think it is perverse to shed tears about the inhumanity of the Jewish Holocaust and overlook at the same time the same inhumanity of the Tibetan Holocaust of today and to continue doing business as usual with these communist murderers. They are no different from the Nazi murderers. Both are, or were, engaged in wiping out a whole culture and a whole people. Some 1,200,000 Tibetans were killed and almost 7,000 monasteries destroyed by the Chinese. Sixty percent of the historical and philosophical libraries of the country were burned; one in ten Tibetans was sent to prison; one third of the country was forcibly incorporated into China, and the rest was declared an "autonomous region" in which 250,000 Red Chinese soldiers forced the Tibetans into camps. There they had to work 14 hours a day and take "re-education" courses which reduced them to machines.

"The true reason for the wave of murders," explained the Dalai Lama, "was the refusal by the Tibetans to renounce their religion; they were not only shot, but beaten to death, crucified, burned alive, drowned, cut into pieces, starved to death, throttled, hung, buried alive or beheaded, their skin was torn off and their limbs amputated. This assassination took place in public before the eyes of the families, friends and neighbors."[7]

An international commission of lawyers confirmed the words of the Dalai Lama and added that children were even forced to shoot their parents. The request by the Dalai Lama before the Chinese invasion in 1959 to bring the case of Tibet before the United Nations was rejected by the governments of the United States, Great Britain and India. You can do research to find out who was in charge of those governments at that time and figure out where your personal responsibility comes in.

Where is the outcry of the media? Where is the compassion for the people involved and where is the intellectual and moral integrity of our leadership to connect and draw conclusions? Are those who play up to totalitarian murderers and defy God representing our best interests? Is Helmuth Kohl, who after all is the head of a Christian party, a Christian? Are Margarete Thatcher or John Major indeed Christians, just because they install the bishops of the Anglican Church? And what about those bishops? Does Bill Clinton represent in his "foreign policy" God's commandment, "Love your neighbor as yourself!"? Should he? And what are you doing about it?

Politicians, across the board, practice internationally what they are practicing at home, they operate on the basis of fiction and make believe, focussing with few or no moral scruples on the short term, normally the election period. Internally they run up unprecedented deficits to pay for their social "compassion" leaving their debts to the next generation. Externally they create totalitarian monsters, leaving the consequences also to the next generation. This certainly is not the way for the leaders (or the led!) to get into the Kingdom of God.

This brings up the question of what the conditions for a government to be righteous are ? Do we have a righteous government in any Western democracy? Is the government of the United States a righteous one and because of it does it have the respect and the allegiance of its law-abiding citizens? Of the nations around the world? My answer is that there is no righteous government in place anywhere in the world. Nowwhere is there that one could call a state of law. We have good laws and bad laws. In America there are still more good ones than in other countries, but the concept is relative and insufficient. There is no universal moral principle at the basis of legislation. Lawmakers, governments and judges manipulate matters according to their own limited understanding of the world.

The French economist, statesman, and author, Frederic Bastiat, stated at the beginning of the 19th century:

> "It is impossible to introduce into society a greater change and a greater evil than this: the conversion of the Law into an instrument of plunder. What are the consequences of such perversion? It would rerquire volumes to describe them all. Thus we must contend ourselves with pointing out the most striking.
>
> In the first place, it erases from everyone's conscience the distinction between justice and injustice. No society can exist unless the laws are respected to a certain degree. The safest way to make laws respected is to make them respectable. When law and morality contradict each other, the citizen has the cruel alternative of either losing his moral sense or losing his respect for the law. These two evils are of equal consequence, and it would be difficult to choose between them. The nature of law is to maintain justice. That is so much the case that, in the minds of the people, law and justice are one and the same thing. There is in all of us a strong disposition to believe that anything lawful is also legitimate."[8]

The truth of this analysis could be seen in Nazi-Germany one hundred years later. The Nazis perverted the law and abandoned the base of absolute morality. Because Germans, not having absolute morality in their personal lives, confused law and legitimacy, the Nazis got away with it. America in the nineties is very advanced on the same road. "Thus, in order to make plunder just and sacred to many consciences," continues Bastiat, "it is only necessary for the law to decree and sanction it."[9]

"But how is this legal plunder to be identified?," he asked, "Quite simply. See if the law takes from some persons what belongs to them, and gives it to other persons to whom it does not belong. See if the law benefits one citizen at the expense of another by doing what the citizen cannot do without committing a crime."[10]

Professor Friedrich A. Hayek, the 1974 joint recipient of the Nobel Peace Prize in Economics stated:

> "Democracy and socialism have nothing in common but one word: equality. But notice the difference: while democracy seeks equality in liberty, socialism seeks equality in restraint and servitude. To allay these suspicions and to harness to its cart the strongest of all political motives - the craving for freedom - socialism began increasingly to make use of the promise of a new freedom.[1] The coming of socialism was to leap from the realm of necessity to the realm of freedom. It was to bring economic freedom,[1] without which the political freedom already gained was not worth having. Only socialism was capable of effecting the consummation of the age-long struggle for freedom, in which the attainment of political freedom was but a first step. The subtle change in meaning to which the word freedom[1] was subjected in order that this argument should sound plausible is important. To the great apostles of political freedom, the word had meant freedom from coercion, freedom from the arbitrary power of other men, release from the ties which left the individual no choice but obedience to the orders of a superior, to whom he was attached. The new freedom, however, was to be freedom from necessity, release from the compulsion of the circumstances which inevitably limit the choice of all of us... Before man could be truly free, the 'despotism of physical want' had to be broken, the 'restraint of the economic system' relaxed." The promise of greater freedom has been a great attraction which drew people to socialist concepts, but "that what was promised to us as the Road to Freedom was in Fact the High Road to Servitude."[11]

Western legislation is riddled with socialist concepts. And when I said earlier that you cannot be a Christian and a Marxist at the same time, I can now additionally state that true patriotism and socialism are mutually exclusive. The question is not bigger or smaller government, but freedom or slavery, because Hayek's *High Road to Serfdom* ends in the totalitarian state. As a matter of fact, it is not going to end there, but will be the transition to self destruction. The German philosopher

Georg Wilhelm Friedrich Hegel explained at the beginning of the nineteenth century that all events in the world are part of the development of the absolute world spirit through the dialectical steps of thesis, anti-thesis to synthesis until the last stage of history and its fullfillment is reached when the spirit of man understands itself. According to Hegel spirit comes before matter.

Marx's historical materialism adopted Hegels dialectic but turned it upside down proclaiming matter to be the cause of spirit. History is understood as the inoxerable march of humanity through a series of class struggles to the classless, communist society where the struggle ends and harmony rules. Each individual is part of this historical process, the marxists(leninists) are the executioners of history and therefore unbeatable in the long run. That concept has not changed through the temporary dissolution of the Soviet Union and it is the historical mission and the all-embracing commitment to it by the standard bearers, not economic abundance or lack of it, which is the driving force of world revolution out to destroy the freedom of man today as then.

Socialists have a global concept, which connects the individual with a program for the world. It ties him in with the history of mankind. Therefore, the answer to communism-socialism ought to be equally within the framework of a realistic global concept and commitment. Christianity, without moral absolutes, has not produced one until now. This is because the concept of the fullfillment of all history in God at the second coming of Jesus Christ remains, in the minds of most sincere Christians, detached from and not related to the social and political power struggle on this earth.

Conservatives from around the world are too narrow minded, selfrighteous and basically limited to their own countries. They don't understand how ridicilous it is to proclaim that capitalism has defeated communism and that the Cold War is over. I can hear Gorbachev and his wife laugh every morning before they meet with or talk to Bush, Thatcher, Kohl, Chirac, Malrony or any other of the ignorant western "conservative" leaders.

Part of what has to be done is to halt power manipulation on all levels, nationally and internationally. "True politics," said the German Pofessor of constitutional law Ernst von Hippel, "does not find justification through its purpose, but must be related to righteousness and evil. It must be in the service of righteousness and if politics loses this relationship, which is a result of the nature of man, then it becomes satanic."[12]

Since the law has a universal character, foreign policy must equally be in the service of righteousness for the benefit of the whole of humanity, explains von Hippel. The individual, as well as any national community, has to be secured against the tyranny of a new superstate. Hippel rejects an omnipotent superstate, or a loose union of 'free nations', but aims at a community of nations of free people.

With Western help, China will in the 21st century be the most powerful nation in the world. That will mean the end of what is left of international law. Arbitrary power will be the rule on the globe exercised on the back of the populations. The World Conference for Human Rights taking place in Vienna in June 1993 elected government representatives of China, Cuba, Syria and Jemen as vice-presidents.

The Dalai Lama of Tibet was excluded from the conference because China made it clear that it did not want him to participate and speak. Western leaders backed down. It is as if Hitler in the thirties would exclude the exiled President of Chechoslovakia, Edvard Benes, from an international conference. All conferences of the United Nations have immorality at their basis. If the United Nations are not liquidated in time, that body will be busy taking money from the "rich" and giving most of it to themselves (and just a little to the "poor" nations), quelling any resistance to their totalitarian control with the troops of the "rich" but inept. They are already doing this. Their programs will be as effecient as the American or European welfare systems of today, and labelled with the same beautiful wordings. You, Christians, are going to pay for all of this with your freedom and your money. It is our responsibility to rise to our feet and take action now.

Britain delivers Hongkong and its population, in good colonial and imperialistic tradition, to totalitarian China. That is a disgrace and an insult to freedom-loving people, but we hear no peep from the rest of the world. It was Winston Churchill who, with a cigar in his mouth and a glass of whisky in his hand, drew the frontier lines across Africa, the Middle East and Eastern Europe on maps before him. He did what he felt was best for British national "interests," creating new countries and eliminating others. Of course he failed to ask the concerned people for their opinions, as little as Lloyd George did thirty-five years earlier. The consequences of such arrogance fell on the following generations, causing unrelenting mutual hatreds, ethnic turmoil and the bloody wars of today in Europe, the Middle East and Africa. The Thatcher government applied the same insane principle to the population of Hong Kong.

Assuming for a moment that the Chinese communist state was a legitimate legal successor to treaties signed by earlier non-communist Chinese governments—which I do not think it is—the fact remains that in the case of Hong Kong the territory the British leased in 1889 from China is only what is called the New Territories with a few of the 236 mostly uninhabited islands. The main bulk of the colony of 411,680 square miles is the island of Hong Kong with the capital Victoria and the peninsula Kowloon. These were not leased and that's where nearly all of the six million people live. China has no legal claim to this part of the Crown-Colony. Nor could it exersise any claim against the will of a population with democratic rights. But the British hypocrites under Margaret Thatcher did not give them any meaningful rights. They did not ask the people what they wanted. Contrary to the principles they claimed in the Falkland Islands war with Argentina, they declared Hong Kong and Kowloon as not viable and threw it all into the totalitarian pot. It interests them as little as the German fellow-Christians cared that the rulers to whom they delivered six million people are the same who are responsible for the Tibetan Holocaust. Shame on Britain! And shame on the West! And shame on sleeping Christians who do not concern themselves!

Global responsibility means looking out for the best interests of other countries too, and those of the other people, contrary to the present practice of manipulating international relations in favor of one's own national advantage (and lying about one's real motivation). It does not matter whether one is dealing with an important big country or an insignifant small one the same principle has to be applied to all: Love your neighbor as you love yourself. That is as difficult for a government as it is for the individual. But doing it in terms of practical policy on the basis of God's moral absolutes means setting one's heart first on the Kingdom of God, aiming at a world where God's justice reigns. It is a job worthy of any politician and nobody will clamor for term limits for statesmen. But it is not an unrealistic dream—it can be and it must be reality. It is the only intelligent long-term policy. It is, in fact, rooted in the best of our values and our traditions, in other words we can be our national selfs: As patriots we cherish and cultivate that and we can and we must take on all the other less-favored nations, as a basis of national policy. That will at the same time free us from the godless socialist redistribution schemes of the United Nations and their like-minded parasitic fellow travellers around the world. Am I, the government, supposed to be my brothers keeper? You bet. Our government's immoral manipulations will not only solve nothing on a long-term basis but will lead us into self-destruction while following the road of God's kingdom will lead us to peace and prosperity.

Selfish people cannot create a new world. Peace does not come by manipulation of and association with immoral government leaders but from inside the people and their leaders. Where there is hatred there is no peace. Peace will always elude us as long as peace to us means only to be left alone in order to be able to look after our own affairs. "First keep peace and order within yourself," said St. Thomas `a Kempis, "then you can create peace and order in others. A person with peace within himself is more useful than somebody with the most extensive learnings."[13] That applies to those foreign secretaries who waste their taxpayers' money travelling around the globe without having anything substantial to say. They only promise money and apply the pressure of material power. "For the Godless are like a raging sea that cannot come to rest and whose waters are full of mud and dirt," says Isaiah. "For the Godless there is no peace, thus sayeth the Lord."[14] Take that literally.

The most pressing need of individuals and humanity today is the necessity for integration, to be at one with life's real purpose, to be at one with your government, to be at one with people and nations around you, to be at one with God and eternity. I do not refer to the socialist multicultural concept which uproots people, destroys traditions and thus makes people tools of godless manipulators. I speak here of the oneness of purpose and of moral standards for all, where individuals become part of their national destiny and we all move with the same purpose toward a world under God, where power is not used for own advantage but for the purposes of our creator. The Catholic theologian, Romano Guardini, points out that the exercise of power over the world must be preceeded by self-renunciation on the part of those who are in positions of power. As he put it, man must come to control his own power. "There can be no rule which is not in the first place rule over oneself..."[15] The purpose of the coming culture is not welfare but power, he explains, "the execution of the instruction which God has planted in the nature of man."[16] "The kingdom of God on earth is the independence of which I dream," said Mahatma Gandhi. "Inner harmony penetrates man`s whole existence. Just as food is indispensible for the body, so prayer is indispensible for the soul. Appearances mean nothing to me. God is truth and the way to Him passes through love."[17] "The aim of the cosmos will have been attained", says Krishna to the warrior Arjuna in the Bhagavadgita, "when the kingdom of God has been established, when existence on this earth is like life in heaven and when all men have attained the wisdom of the spirit."[18]

"The purpose of life," says the British theologian J.B. Philips, is "the gradual winning of man to a willing loyalty to ... establishing the rule of God."[19] That is the ultimate destiny of every human being and of every government. The issue for humanity at this late hour is its destiny, to find the reason for being. Presidential candidates, by the way, had better pay attention as does Alan Keyes.

Our destiny comes from God. America, as a nation, was given its destiny at birth. It has deviated, and needs to get back on course. It is the egos of the good people which stand in the way of unity of purpose and action. Many will have to crucify their egos, so that America will find its destiny. Everyone who loves his country will have to connect with the power of God. Let me summarize the steps to be taken in order to switch on the light:

1. Stop blaming others for the hard times you are suffering and for the bad things you are doing.

2. Look closely at yourself and your motives.

3. Turn to God and clean your life.

4. Make restitution.

5. Listen to God on a regular basis; write down your own thoughts.

6. Follow His guidance. Faith is a consequence of obedience.

7. Fight for moral change in others and in society.

8. Fight for moral change and vision in your political leadership.

9. Make the Kingdom of God the priority in all you do and desire.

10. Don't be disheartened if you make mistakes or things don't turn out the way you thought. Keep at it.

REFERENCES

Chapter One: PREPARING THE ARGUMENT
1. Romans 2, 14 - 16
2. Ed Miller: God and Reason, p. 212
3. Same: p. 153

Chapter Four: GOD'S GUIDANCE
1. John Hick (ed.): Classical and Contemporary Readings in the Philosophy of Religion, p. 118
2. Ed Miller: God and Reason, p. 72, quoted from David Hume, "The natural history of religion", ed. H.E. Root, Stanford University Press 1956, p.76
3. Same, p. 72/73, quoted from "Why I Am Not a Christian, and Other Essays, ed. Paul Edwards (New York: Simon & Schuster 1957
4. Thomas von Kempen: Das Buch von der Nachfolge Christi, p.92 - book 3, chapter 1ts

Chapter Five: GOD AND JOB SECURITY
1. St. John 18, 37
2. St. John 18, 39

Chapter Six: GOD AND SOCIETY
1. Criticon 146, April/June 1995, p.74 (German news magazine)
2. Aida Parker Newsletter, Issue No. 176, September 1994
3. John Barron: KGB, p.139

4. Ulrich Hoever: Joseph Goebbels - ein nationaler Sozialist, quoted in the review by Manfred Funke in the "Frank furter Allgemeine Zeitung, April 22, 1994

5. Alexander Solzhenitsyn (ed.): From Under the Rubble, p.274

6. Vaclav Havel: Versuch, in der Wahrheit zu leben, p.34

7. The News (Mexico), November 27, 1987

8. Max Weber: Soziologie—Universalgeschichtliche Analysen—Politik, p. 380

9. Samuel Igra: Germany's National Vice, p.73

Chapter 8: GOD OR IDOLS

1. Thomas von Kempen: Das Buch von der Nachfolge Christi, p.10

2. Isaiha 44, 18

3. Isaiha 66, 4

4. Isaiha, 8

Chapter Nine: Taking the Sins of your Nation upon Yourself

1. Joachim C. Fest: Hitler, p.21

Chapter 10: Set Your Heart First on the Kingdom of God

1. St. Matthew 6, 33

2. St. Matthew 6, 25

3. Luke 17, 21

4. Scott M. Peck: The Road Less Traveled, p. 312

5. Same, p.281

6. Same, p.283

7. Dalai Lama: Mein Leben und mein Volk, p.175

8. Frederic Bastiat: The Law, p.12-13

9. Same, p.13

10. Same, p. 21

11. Friedrich von Hayek: The Road to Serfdom, p.25-26

12. Ernst von Hippel: Mechanisches und Moralisches Rechtsdenken, p.177

13. Thomas von Kempen: Das Buch von der Nachfolge Christi, p.67
14. Isaiha 57, 20-21
15. Roman Guardini: Die Macht, p.126
16. Same, p. 106
17. Gandhi Muesuem, New Delhi, India.
18. Bhagavadgita
19. J.B. Phillips: Your God is too Small, p.90

BIBLIOGRAPHY

Augustinus, "Der Gottesstaat (De Civitate Dei)", Johannes Verlag, Einsiedeln 1961

Barron, John, "KGB", Bantam Books, New York 1974

Bastiat Frederic, "The Law", The Foundation For Economic Education, Irvington-on-Hudson 1993

Bradley Francis, "The American Proposition", Moral Re-Armament, New York 1977

Dalai Lama, "Mein Leben und mein Volk", Droemersche Verlagsanstalt, München 1962

Dalai Lama, "Freedon in Exile", Harper Collins, New York 1990

Fest Joachim C., "Hitler", Ullstein, Berlin 1983

Funderburk, David B., "The Betryal of America", The Larry Mcdonald Foundation, Dunn 1991

Guardini Romano, "Die Macht", Werkbund Verlag, Würzburg 1957

Havel Vaclav, "Versuch, in der Wahrheit zu Leben", Rohwolt, Reinbeck 1990

Hayek Friedrich A. von, "The Road to Serfdom", The University of Chicago Press, Chicago 1972

Hick John, (editor), "Classical and Contemporary Readings in the Philosophy of Religion", Prentice-Hall, Englewood Cliffs 1990

Hippel Ernst von, "Mechanisches und Moralisches Rechtsdenken", Anton Hain, Meisenheim 1959

Hoever Ulrich, "Joseph Goebbels - ein nationaler Sozialist", Bouvier Verlag, Bonn/Berlin 1992

Igra Samuel, "Germany's National Vice", Quality Press, London 1945

Kempis Thomas A., "Das Buch von der Nachfolge Christi" (The Book about Following Christ), Reclam Stuttgart 1954

Lively Scott and Abrams Kelly, "The Pink Swastika", Founders Publishing Corporation, Keizer, Oregon 1995

Manstein Erich von, "Verlorene Siege", Atheneum-Verlag, Bonn 1955

Miller Ed, "God and Reason", Macmillan, New York 1972

Noebel David A., "Understanding the Times", Summit Press, Manitou Springs 1991

Peck M. Scott, "The Road Less Traveled", Simon and Schuster, New York 1978

Peck M. Scott, "People of the Lie", Simon and Schuster, New York 1983

Phillips J.B., "Your God is too Small", Macmillan, New York 1961

Ravines Eudocio, "The Yenan Way", Charles Scribner's Sons, New York 1951

Smith Earl E.T., "The Fourth Floor", Selous Foundation, Washington D.C. 1987

Solzhenitsyn Alexander, "From Under The Rubble", Little Brown, Boston 1974

Stahlberg Alexander, "Die Verdammte Pflicht", Ullstein, Berlin 1987

Weber Max, "Soziologie - Universalgeschichtliche Analysen Politik", Alfred Kroener Verlag, Stuttgart 1973

The Bhagavad Gita, translation from Sanskrit by Juan Mascar, Penguin Books, New York 1987

The New Testament in modern English, translated by J.B. Phillips, Collier Books (Macmillan), New York

ANOTHER BOOK BY THE AUTHOR:

MORAL MELTDOWN

THE CORE OF GLOBALISM

A POLITICAL ANALYSIS OF GLOBAL ISSUES

HUNTINGTON HOUSE PUBLISHERS

1-800-749-4009

P.O. BOX 53788 - LAFAYETTE, LA 70505